Consciously Parenting:

What it *Really* Takes
to Raise Emotionally Healthy Families

By Rebecca Thompson, M.S.

Published in the United States by
The Consciously Parenting Project, LLC

Paperback Version
Original Source: Consciously Parenting:
What It Really Takes to Raise Emotionally Healthy Families
March 2012 edition
ISBN: 978-0-9842756-2-5

Original Process: The Consciously Parenting Project, LLC
Created by: The Consciously Parenting Project, LLC

Illustrations by: Susan Graham
Book Design by: Lianne March

Special thanks to Shannon Livingston of Livingston Galleries
for the cover photo. http://www.shannonlivingston.com

View My Website:
http://www.consciouslyparenting.com
http://www.holisticfamilyconsultant.com
E-mail me: rebecca@consciouslyparenting.com

For Ryan, Zack, and Josh, with gratitude for your love, your support, and for sharing the journey. And for Jacob.

Without you and all you've taught me, this book would not have been possible.

With appreciation:

I am so very grateful for all the support I've had over the years it has taken me to write this book from many, many people. Without all the encouragement, support while scribbling on napkins, and listening to me talk endlessly about these ideas, this would simply not have been possible. I would need to write another book to thank everyone adequately, but I'll do my best in the space I have.

Special thanks to Lianne March, without whom The Consciously Parenting Project and this book would not have been possible. Thank you for seeing the vision and helping me to make all this a reality, for late night e-mails and brainstorms. You have my heartfelt thanks.

Amy Rost, the best book midwife ever. Thank you for your time, your attention, your passion, and going above and beyond the call of duty to help breathe life and clarity into this book.

With appreciation to Bethany Shetler, Wilma Vance, Sally Flintoff, MaryJo McHaney, Ammana Shaka, and Valerie Groves for your encouragement, your wisdom, and your passion for families who have adopted or fostered children. Your contributions to the earliest versions of this book were essential to its development.

To my friends who supported and encouraged me through the ups and downs of writing and life: Susan Graham, my cruising buddy, for your saint-like support and willingness to listen and wait, and to draw on napkins and other table coverings with me. Debra Hart for living life on the other side of the worm hole, for reminding me to sing, for your honesty and clarity. Lu Hanessian for helping me remember why I'm doing this, for seeing what others couldn't see, for belly laughs and pillow fights. Janet Conner for providing so much more than a space to write.

For professional inspiration that has deeply affected my work, thank you to Pam Leo, Ray Castellino, Mary Jackson, Lu Hanessian, Suzanne Arms, and Carrie Contey. Thank you for lighting the way for so many families around the world.

Special thanks to my book readers. I appreciate your feedback to help make this book user-friendly: Erika S., Evelyn K., Lisa, Debra and Riley, David and Fran, Lianne, Ellen O., Becca, Janet, Lisa W., Tiffany C., Theresa, Sally, Bethany, MaryJo, Wilma.

I am eternally grateful to all the families I've worked with over the years who have taught me so much about life, love, and the importance of remaining open and curious about ourselves and our loved ones. It isn't always the journey we thought we were going on, but it is the journey we were meant to make.

Rebecca Thompson, MS, MFT
Crystal Beach, FL
March, 2012

Contents

**Chapter Six:
How We Interpret Our Children's Behavior**

Principle 5: Parental interpretation of behaviors comes from both a conscious and subconscious place, resulting in positive or negative neurophysiologic feedback loops.

**Chapter Seven: Feelings:
Messages from Our Internal Guidance System**

Principle 6: All individuals have a right and a responsibility to learn to express their feelings appropriately. Feelings allow us to connect to our internal guidance system.

**Chapter Eight:
Setting Limits While Honoring Feelings**   113

Principle 7: Children need boundaries. We can set appropriate limits for our children while still respecting their needs and feelings—if we are aware of ourselves. (We can ask, for example, "Is this about me? Is this about them? Are my children communicating a need? Is the boundary I'm setting necessary, or is it an opportunity for me to grow?")

Chapter Nine:
Connecting in Community, Connecting to Ourselves 128

Principle 8: No man is an island. We need to create communities of support for ourselves and for our children. We need to take care of ourselves so that we can take care of our children.

Introduction

Pick up any parenting book, and you're likely to be confronted with a list of children's behaviors and a corresponding list of things the parent can do to supposedly make the behaviors go away. Parents spend millions of dollars on quick fixes—books and devices that promise their child will sleep through the night, improve in school, or move out of the house in a timely manner. Many of these resources promise short-term solutions without looking at the long-term relationship between a parent and child. Unfortunately, many parenting books are not based upon science, nor are they based upon relationship. And science and intuition have both told us that there is nothing more important than relationship. Most parenting information aims to make behaviors that we don't like go away, rather than looking at the long-term consequences of how we're attempting to change those behaviors and what those attempts will do to the relationship over the long haul.

Standard parenting advice leads parents down the path of disconnection rather than connection in relationships. Disconnection is rampant in our society, particularly with the consistent focus on children's behaviors and making specific behaviors go away. With the amount of stress in the daily lives of most U.S. families, today's family members have more trouble connecting with each other than family members of the past did. We have multiple opportunities every day to connect with our children, yet instead we often choose to connect with technology (phones, televisions, and computers, just to name a few). It isn't that we don't love our children or we don't want to be with them. In fact, most parents want to connect with their children. Perhaps we just don't know how to connect in a deep, meaningful way. In addition, our families are also quite isolated from other families, and we do not have the same community for raising our children as past generations commonly did. When you talk to many young parents, their feeling of being overwhelmed is palpable—and for good reason.

Parenting actually isn't about waiting for children to outgrow this stage or that stage, or finding the right gadget or gimmick to make their negative behaviors disappear. It is a long-term process of relationship, of attunement, of getting to know your child and getting to know yourself. We all want good relationships with our children, but we are often unsure what these relationships look like or how to get to them from where we are right now. If you're ready to dig a little deeper and understand the foundation of good parent-child relationships, including your relationships with your own children, how to create and nurture healthy parent-child relationships, and how to repair those relationships in a state of disconnection, you're in the right place! This book examines the science of parenting, because we actually do know what children need for optimal development. This book is also a compilation of what I've learned on my own parenting journey and from my work with hundreds of families over the past twenty years in various capacities; they and my children and husband have all taught me so much about family, relationships, and connection.

Who Is a Parent?

Author's note: The term parent, as used in this book, refers to any adult who serves as a child's primary caregiver, regardless of if or how that adult is biologically related to the child.

My Story

When I was growing up, my parents struggled to find peace. Much of the time, chaos ruled in the house I grew up in, and my parents sought out expert after expert to figure out what they could change to bring things under control. They tried to control every single behavior of their three children in an attempt to create some semblance of order. For example, when I was in high school, my parents found a therapist who suggested behavior-controlling techniques such as "chair," which was a humiliating version of "timeout" for teenagers. Whenever one of us children did something our parents didn't like, such as talking back or even trying to clarify something that happened that they didn't want to hear, we were forced to sit in a chair in the center of the living room; while sitting there, we were unable to talk, sometimes for an hour or more. But nothing they tried worked. I watched as my younger brother became adept at sneaking out of windows to be with his friends, while my youngest brother spiraled into a depression. And I, who felt completely disconnected from everyone, became more shut down and isolated.

The therapist's efforts to "help" us culminated in my parents sending both of my brothers to a hospital's residential treatment center—a last ditch effort to scare us into total compliance with their wishes and rules. Resentment grew in our entire family along with the pain we experienced. Instead of just living in a state of chaos, we now hated each other and our lives. Everyone was miserable. I started counting down the days until I would be able to leave for college, isolating myself in my room whenever possible. I did not share any of my concerns with my parents, and I got to the point that I could rarely even share with my friends what was happening in my family or in my life. I felt that reaching out only brought more pain and suffering, and just keeping quiet, not drawing any unnecessary attention to myself, was the way to survive until I could be out on my own. When I had children of my own, I resolved, I would not struggle so much. I knew the pain of the path my parents had gone down, and I was determined to create a new path for myself and for my family.

When I finally went off to college to study elementary education, I had a course in behavioral psychology. I readily identified it as the theory behind the suggestions the (misguided) therapist had given to my parents when I was a teenager. I saw how the theory focused only on a child's behavior, and I felt a cry from my soul: What about the intention of the behavior? What about how the child feels? What about trying to understand the child and helping him or her feel safe? What about the parent-child relationship? When the professor brought in puppies and asked us to do whatever it took to get our assigned puppy to comply with our wishes, I knew that this theory was missing something critically important. The exercise with a furry pet was meant to prepare us teachers in training to manage our future classrooms and the young children in our care, but I knew people and relationships are much more complex than this exercise led us to believe. I knew there must be another way of looking at children and their behaviors. I suspected it had something to do with respecting children's feelings, but I wasn't yet sure what that might look like.

When I became a parent myself, I was amazed at how much information focused on a child's behaviors. Because of my experiences in childhood, I was looking for information that explained what I saw in my own home growing up and would help me avoid those same pitfalls. Pieces began to come together for me with the practice of attachment parenting (AP) and its focus on the connection in my relationship with my son Zack. It felt good. And it was healing. I knew there was nothing more important than our relationship, and the needs my son expressed told me which way to go. I felt beyond the shadow of a doubt that I was moving in the right direction, confident that I had averted the disasters and rampant disconnection that had happened in my own childhood.

Then tragedy and a new set of lessons entered my life. It was 2002—probably the worst year of my life. That was the year my newborn son, Jacob, died, and three-and-a-half-year-old Zack's behaviors changed into something I did not understand. I was overwhelmed in every sense of the word. I read every parenting book that I could find, and nothing seemed to help. Desperate, I found myself trying all those things that my own parents had resorted to—timeouts, punishments, rewards, ignoring my son when he acted inappropriately, yelling at him— until I finally resorted to letting him just watch television all day because I didn't know what else to do. When I went out for a while, he panicked. What did that mean in a child who was nearly four years old? He had temper tantrums over everything, and they seemed to grow worse by the day. The books I read didn't help—they only seemed to confuse me more. And none of them seemed to address the root of the problem or to touch me in a way that indicated I was on the right path. But still, I had to be the parent, and somehow I made it through that year. And the next. And the next. And the next.

I thought it would get better as Zack grew older. Certainly these behaviors were something he would outgrow, right? But as the years went by and the angry outbursts grew worse, I felt more and more like a failure as a mother. My marriage wasn't in good place, either, at the time, so I felt like I was just failing everyone, especially myself. This just wasn't how life as a parent was supposed to be. I had planned my children, going to therapy before I even conceived because I knew that parenting might be rough for me given my early history of chaos. I earned a degree in marriage and family therapy, learned about attachment theory and the impact of trauma, and did my best to parent in a con-nected and loving way. My oldest was a high-need child right from day one, but I always made sure that I met his needs because I understood that I was creating patterns that would last him a lifetime. And we had been very connected—at least until 2002, when my baby died.

It sounds funny to say this now, but I didn't fully understand how deeply my second child's death affected me. I didn't know that I responded to extreme stress by shutting down, and I didn't know that shutting down and disconnecting were the very things that were escalating my son's behaviors. Some lessons are more difficult than others, and a lesson will be repeated until learned. The lessons grew harder and harder, but I still didn't know how to do things differently.

In the meantime, I continued to help other families create connections with their young children, knowing full well that I was somehow disconnected from my own child and didn't know how to change that. When families who had started out well but had derailed for some reason came to me, I had no idea how to help them get back to that place of connection. It was an awful feeling.

Over the next few years, I met a series of people who reminded me that the way out wasn't through more disconnection, but through connection. It was through other people loving me right where I was that I was able to see that my son needed nothing more than for me to love him right where he was—in the midst of his pain and his fear. Yes, this child who seemed to deserve love the least needed it the most.

My son couldn't change his behaviors until I changed mine. When I was reacting to his behaviors, I was operating at the same level of consciousness as my four-year-old. In fact, many of our behaviors were very similar. I had to return to focusing on attachment and our connection to each other. I found that my own early experiences made it difficult to simply follow my intuition and know the way to go, so I needed others who could remind me to take the road of higher consciousness. This journey to a higher consciousness was going to provide more healing for me and allow me to directly address the pain of my own past.

Problems are not solved by blaming others, as I had learned in therapy before I had my son, but by looking at our own part in creating the problem. I realized that we can learn so much about ourselves by observing how we behave with other people, especially our children. Parenting was an opportunity to learn more about my own early patterns, as Harville Hendrix suggests in his book *Keeping the Love You Find*. I felt hope for the first time in many years. I had no idea what kind of journey I was setting out on; I knew only that it was my journey to make and that learning to reconnect with my son was the first thing that, in many years, felt right deep within my soul regarding the direction of my parenting. I was ready to do whatever it took to change.

The Courage to Change

Many people decide that the way they were parented is not how they would like to parent their own children. However, as their children grow, they may find themselves falling into their parents' old patterns. Patterns of relationship, for better or for worse, are passed from generation to generation unless we parents are willing to look closer and decide to make them different. Before we can make lasting changes in our relationships, we need to first become aware of our patterns of relationship and bring them into our consciousness. It is only then can we become conscious parents and parent consciously. To paraphrase Albert Einstein, "A problem cannot be solved at the same level of consciousness at which it was created." Creating a new reality takes shifting the way we look at our children and their behaviors, along with how we look at ourselves and interpret our own behaviors.

Change also takes perseverance, dedication, commitment to following through, and returning to a focus on the relationship when the going gets tough. Changing how you parent is not a one-time decision to do something differently; it is a process, not an event. It takes forgiving yourself when you don't parent perfectly—and you won't. But imperfect parenting and forgiving yourself are part of the process. The process includes admitting that you didn't handle something the way you wanted, forgiving yourself, and asking your child to forgive you. Pam Leo, in her book *Connection Parenting,* suggests that parents model for their children a process of rewind, repair, and replay, for these are the very things we want our children to be able to do. Simply, Pam is talking about going back into what just happened, apologizing for our part, creating space for our child's feelings, and then trying it again the way we wanted it to go.

Becoming a conscious parent is also about sticking with connection and relationship when the going gets tough, and it is about the power of unconditional love for both parents and for child. There is nothing more important than connected relationships.

Beginning the Journey of Change

Every journey begins with the first step, and the first step of this journey is education. With a new understanding of relationships; a simple, 101-level course in brain science; and a look at how to apply the ideas, you'll be on your way to a different kind of relationship with your child and within your family.

First, I'm going to give you some information that, unlike most of the parenting information out there, is grounded in science and research. Most of the popular parenting "techniques" are based on dated information and are counterproductive to helping your child grow into a well-balanced, emotionally healthy individual. The vast majority of the parenting techniques are strictly behavioral, and they neglect or negate the vital importance of relationships and emotional connections in healthy development. Having the correct information about our children's development is absolutely essential to making informed parenting decisions, because the choices that we make as parents give us much power (and with that, much responsibility) and more influence over our children's overall mental and emotional health than over any other factor. Multiple areas of study, from divergent fields—such as pre- and perinatal psychology, neuroscience, biology, trauma research, anthropology, and others—are coming together to validate the importance of emotional regulation and connection in optimal human development. Conscious parenting isn't a technique or something prescriptive, but rather a process of creating connection from where you are right now.

I will also provide examples from real families who have had real struggles, just like yours, and show you different ways of looking at your child's behaviors, which will create understanding and build your relationship.

In Book I, we will look at the foundation of relationships, including attachment and the impact of our early relationships on who we become. In Book II, we will look at how we create healthy relationships. In Book III, our focus shifts to how we can nurture healthy relationships, which includes looking at ages and stages of development. In Book IV, we'll look at repairing relationships and how we can create connection where there has been a trauma or other disconnection in a relationship. All of the relationship information focuses on the parent-child relationship, though you'll quickly see that it applies to all relationships.

We need some basic tools on this journey, and this book will give you a template to create those tools for your family. But I'm not here to tell you what to do in every situation. There are no one-size-fits-all answers here. Each situation and each family is unique, and there is no single right answer. I'm not here to be just another "expert," but to enable you to quickly become your own expert. You will become an expert of your own life, empowered to find solutions that go beyond trying to change your child's behaviors and are based on what truly matters: building connected, trusting family relationships and bonds that can weather any situation.

Parenting can truly be a healing journey, if we allow it to be. And our children can be our best teachers, helping us to see those parts of ourselves that need healing. I have seen it happen over and over again in families that previously had no hope, including my own.

Parents all over the world are taking bold steps to set aside the traditional views about children and reach beyond it for something deeper and much more fully connected to both their children and to themselves. If you are willing to consider this possibility, I invite you to come along on a parenting journey that will open you up to new connections with your family and with yourself. Join the growing group of parents around the globe as we all move toward peace, harmony, joy, unconditional love, and unconditional acceptance of ourselves and of each other. Join us on this great adventure of parenting with connection, of learning more about yourself and reawakening to your true self. It will be the best investment you'll ever make!

Book I

The Foundation of the
Parent-Child Relationship

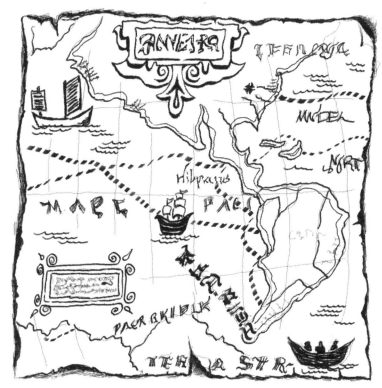

Chapter One

Your Compass and Map:
Inner Guidance and Guiding Principles

My Own Journey Begins

When I was working on my master's degree in marriage and family therapy, I found myself drawn to the literature about trauma. Most of it was about military veterans, as they had the most clearly defined traumas and their large groups made the effects of those traumas easy to study. Even though I'm not a veteran, I found the information to be fascinating. It seemed strange that something that happened to you a long time ago could still affect you on a daily basis. How did that happen? Why did that happen?

What really stuck with me was that even when a group of soldiers experienced an identical traumatic experience, such as a catastrophic explosion, only about half developed long-term symptoms of distress. What made the difference? Turns out the answer could be found in what happened in the soldier's first three years of life, specifically in the bond that forms between parent and child due to appropriate and adequate caregiving. This bond, or the lack thereof, affects the way that people view the world and how they ultimately handle their biggest stressors.

In 1997 I went to the American Association for Marriage and Family Therapy conference in Atlanta and attended a preconference session on attachment and trauma, led by Susan M. Johnson from Canada. Johnson had developed a treatment protocol for creating attachment relationships to heal trauma; this treatment was called emotion-focused therapy. Most of the time, she was using the marital relationship to create healing connection that would help people recover from the effects of trauma. The healing had far-reaching ramifications for one or both of the individuals in the relationship; it gave the trauma-tized individual relief from his or her symptoms and allowed for deeper connection to the self, and it also had a positive effect on the marriage.

Johnson said that those who hadn't received positive care and attention from parents or other caregivers as babies and young children didn't learn to reach out to others at times of distress. If something distressing happened when these people were older, they tended to keep both details of the distressing experience and the feelings about it to themselves, because they had learned from their early experiences that reaching out would only bring them more pain. So it was better to just keep the details and feelings inside. Johnson explained that it was the ability to reach out during times of distress that made the difference between those who developed post-traumatic stress disorder (PTSD) and those who didn't.

A year after attending Johnson's seminar, I was expecting my first baby. As I was preparing for the birth of my son, I started to read more about attachment. If this concept was indeed as important as Johnson had said it was, then I wanted to be as proactive as possible.

I read a lovely book by Robert Karen called *Becoming Attached: Unfolding the Mystery of the Mother-Infant Bond.* I was mesmerized. It cited so many interesting studies that showed how important the mother, or the primary attachment figure, is to the developing child. The bond that developed between the child and this person could make the difference between a child doing well in life and not. Creating and nurturing a powerful connection with your child was one of the most important tasks of parenthood! I had had no idea.

I decided to do an Internet search to see what was written about attachment theory and parenting, and through it I learned of a pediatrician named William Sears, who had coined the term *attachment parenting*. And there were many resources on attachment available. I began to read books about co-sleeping (something that I had said I would *never* do), making my own baby food, using cloth diapers, breastfeeding, using a sling, and not leaving my baby to cry alone.

I planned for a birth outside the hospital and assisted by midwives. I read *The Continuum Concept* by Jean Liedloff, *The Family Bed* by Tine Thevenin, *Three in a Bed* by Deborah Jackson, *The Womanly Art of Breastfeeding* published by La Leche League, and anything by Sears.

After my baby was born, I began to feel alone in my parenting decisions. I saw that the moms I had connected with during my pregnancy were not doing the things these books advocated. They were letting their babies "cry it out," to teach the children to sleep on their own. They were leaving their babies to go on cruises. They were feeling very angry if their babies weren't eating and sleeping when Mom thought they should, and they were using bottles and formula instead of breastfeeding. I felt very alone and isolated. Was I the only person who knew how important the mother was to her baby? Was I the only person who was really looking at my parenting choices in an objective way and not simply doing what my parents did or what those around me were doing? I know now that I wasn't, but it certainly felt that way at the time. I supposed there has always been a part of me that has danced to a different drumbeat, but it was never more obvious than when I became a mother.

I started asking lots of questions: What was love? How do parents show that they love their children while still being the parents? What was attachment? What was bonding? How was I supposed to do those things? What parental behaviors lead to the best outcomes for children? Did it matter that I had trauma as a part of my life's story? What was I supposed to do about all of those little behaviors that I didn't like coming from my son? Why did other parents seem to have areas where they couldn't meet their child's needs, even if they knew intellectually that there was a better way? I seemed to have no guiding compass other than the simple desire to meet my son's needs. That was better than nothing, but I soon found out it wasn't enough.

As I began to parent my own son, I realized that my own past experiences, along with my husband's differing experiences, created an interesting mix of indecision and conflict about the best path for our family regarding parenting. I had my "head" learning, but I wasn't sure in my heart what was right beyond holding my baby son and meeting his expressed needs. I wasn't sure how to handle the conflict that had developed in my marriage, and it seemed I had to choose between the baby's needs and my husband's needs, which didn't feel right. As I started to look around at other parents, I realized that almost all parents were struggling to some degree, especially as they were raising their first child, with what they wanted to do and what kind of parent they wanted to be.

Navigating by Inner Guidance

Now, as then, so many families are still struggling, and parents don't know what to do. Many parents have gone from expert to expert only to find themselves back in the same place or in a worse place than they were before they followed the "expert" advice. At a very early age, most of us learned that the answers are outside of ourselves, and so we seek external solutions to our problems. We think that someone else is going to come and save us.

Part of the problem is that we're afraid to not follow the advice of someone who seems to know what they're talking about. Even when something about a piece of "expert" advice doesn't feel right to us, we disregard that still, small voice within us, and things get worse. Or while we may know intuitively that something isn't right or makes no sense, we don't know what to do instead. In the past, much of the parenting information out there has been conflicting at best and misleading and damaging to relationships at worst. We've all heard so much information about parenting that we don't know what is really correct anymore.

That's where I found myself as a parent. I was listening to my heart and doing the best I could with the information I had, but it wasn't working. I simply didn't know where else to turn or what else to do to help my family out of the rut we were in on all levels.

Eventually, I realized the solutions to all the things we struggle with personally and as parents can be found inside us. Like the way back to Kansas was for Dorothy in *The Wizard of Oz*, what we're seeking can be found within. The difficulties our children present to us are opportunities for us to grow beyond where we are in this moment. My child wasn't trying to manipulate me, but he was providing me with an opportunity to grow and learn. Parenting our own children provides a unique opportunity to learn about our early experiences. It puts a magnifying glass on those things that worked well for our own parents and those that didn't. It allows us to understand how we feel about our own needs and the needs of our children, but only if we allow ourselves to be aware and see the parent-child relationship with new eyes.

Truly connecting with our children takes waking up, stepping into full consciousness, and reconnecting with ourselves and our own inner wisdom. It will probably be one of the most difficult things we will ever do, but it is also one of the most rewarding. I know firsthand that finding your own voice can feel daunting. Like stepping off the shore into the ocean, we must first go through the crashing surf before we reach the calmer, gently rolling waves on the other side. Everything becomes easier when we have passed through the rough water and found that we can handle what floats our way. However, it isn't always an easy journey. Storms are bound to come up and test our ability to stay connected to ourselves in this new way. Indeed, parenting in this manner is a journey, not a tropical island destination at which we arrive with our luggage and simply unpack and settle in with a frosty tropical beverage, happy kids in tow.

We're going to start with you, and you will be modeling what it looks like to stay connected to yourself. By doing so, your children will learn to connect to their own inner guidance rather than looking at external sources to find answers. Your children are going to be on their own at some point, out in the big, wide world without you. Helping them find their own internal compass is one of the best things you can do to help them prepare for the real world. In Book III, we'll take a look at what navigating by internal compass looks like at each developmental stage. (And these developmental stages are based on a child's emotional or developmental age, rather than chronological age.)

With our parenting decisions, we have the power to create connection instead of disconnection, love instead of fear, peace instead of discord. Then we can return to our natural "perfect" state of harmony, peace, and joy.

Inner Guidance and Consciously Parenting

When we grow up and become parents ourselves, our ability to cope with stressful situations is strongly influenced by how connected we are to our inner guidance and how behavior focused we are. Unfortunately, most of us start our lives being parented with behavior-focused strategies aimed to get us to stop doing what "they" didn't want us to do *or* to make us do what "they" wanted us to do. Depending upon lots of factors, these strategies either scared us into submission and disconnected us from ourselves and our inner guidance, or they caused us to push back against the attempt to control our behavior but left us feeling that we were "bad" for doing so. Sometimes it was a combination of both outcomes over time. If we pushed back, we may have still been connected to ourselves, but probably no longer trusted our inner wisdom because it wasn't respected by those who cared for us. Signs that we're disconnected from our inner guidance system include unhappiness, disempowerment, physical ailments and pains, malaise, yearning for love, and emotional diagnoses, such as depression or attention deficit disorder (ADD).

When we disconnect from our inner guidance, we go back into autopilot and naturally do what was done to us, using behavior-focused, fear-based strategies that create disconnection in our relationships with our children. In essence, we are living unconsciously. When we're not fully conscious, we're stuck with only those things that have been said and done to us, along with what society says.

Go within yourself and connect back to your true self, the beautiful soul you are. Find and connect with the beauty in your children—not in what they do, but who they are. When you connect to yourself and your children, you can connect in relationship, because you are fully present in it, perhaps for the very first time. Solutions you couldn't see before suddenly appear before you, and you see everything with new eyes. You are now parenting consciously!

Inner guidance doesn't have formulaic solutions, but always comes back to connecting with your children in relationship, holding the importance of everyone's needs whenever possible.

The Difference Between Unconscious and Conscious Parenting

Unconscious Parenting: "Us versus them" mindset; formulas for changing behaviors; fear-based control; disconnection from ourselves and/or our children; needs and feelings seen as inconvenient and generally not relevant to behavior (ours or our children's).

Conscious Parenting: Finding our way together through our relationship; infinite possibilities and solutions; loving, relationship-focused, connection to ourselves and our inner guidance system; needs and feelings seen as part of the experience and communication; harmony, peace, and joy!

Guiding Principles of Conscious Parenting

While we want to use our inner compass to keep ourselves on course, it also helps to know where we're going. For that, a road map is essential, and for ours, we'll be using eight guiding principles of conscious parenting.

Principle 1: All behavior is a communication. Behavior reflects the internal state of the individual and the relationship's level of connection.

Principle 2: The parent-child relationship is more important than any behavioral intervention, consequence, or punishment.

Principle 3: Children unfold neurosequentially, and quality, connected relationships allow for the unfolding. A need met will go away; a need unmet is here to stay.

Principle 4: Behaviors occur on a continuum. Behaviors in children (and parents, too) correlate to the parents' own neuro-development and attachment status.

Principle 5: Parental interpretation of behaviors comes from both a conscious and subconscious place, resulting in positive or negative neurophysiologic feedback loops.

Principle 6: All individuals have a right and a responsibility to learn to express their feelings appropriately. Feelings allow us to connect to our internal guidance system.

Principle 7: Children need boundaries. We can set appropriate limits for our children while still respecting their needs and feelings—if we are aware of ourselves. (We can ask, for example, "Is this about me? Is this about them? Are my children communicating a need? Is the boundary I'm setting necessary, or is this situation an opportunity for me to grow?")

Principle 8: No man is an island. We need to create communities of support for ourselves and for our children. We need to take care of ourselves so that we can take care of our children.

The following chapters take an in-depth look at each of these principles, explaining how we currently view situations and how to start making the shift toward loving connection. Those who are just starting this journey will be able to start creating connection with their children from the beginning. But no matter where you currently are on the road, you can start to change from disconnection to loving connection.

Eight Guiding Principles of Conscious Parenting:

A Keyword Summary

1. Communication
2. Relationship
3. Unfolding
4. Parent behavior

5. Interpretation
6. Feelings
7. Boundaries
8. Community and self-care

Chapter Two

What Is Your Child's Behavior Saying?

Principle 1: All behavior is a communication. Behavior reflects the internal state of the individual and the relationship's level of connection.

The shoe went flying through the air right at me. I had to duck to avoid it. It wasn't a flip-flop, but a huge mountain boot (mine), and the boy throwing it was my eight-year-old son. I had been his target, and this wasn't a playful game. His behavior was clearly communicating something about his internal state and our relationship. My first interpretation, which happened in an instant, was, "I can't let him get away with that!" My actions reflected this interpretation as I walked toward him, trying to tower over him and let him know how much throwing heavy boots at me wasn't OK. Before I got there, another boot came flying in my direction. What was I going to do to make this different? How do you connect with *that?!*

At that moment, all I knew was that what I'd been doing as a parent wasn't working, and I needed to start somewhere. I needed a new vocabulary and a new way of explaining what I was seeing, to shift from a focus on my son's behavior to the connection in our relationship.

Regulation and Dysregulation

Regulation and *dysregulation*—we use these terms to describe the internal state of an individual. In the past, if someone was dysregulated, we might have labeled that person *angry, manipulative,* or *a brat,* and applied other terms I won't put into print. Their outward behaviors reflect their disturbed internal state— one they can't often articulate clearly. Dysregulation happens when someone experiences stress beyond what he or she can cope with alone. In contrast, when someone is regulated, he or she is experiencing an internal state of calm. The term *regulation* is used in every scientific discipline and is strongly correlated to overall mental health, yet it is a term most parents have never heard before.

To make the difference between regulation and dysregulation easy to understand, let's compare our internal states to a stoplight. When we see a green traffic light, we know we're free to drive right on through the intersection. The green-light state is the calm state of regulation. When we're in this state, we're operating primarily from the conscious, rational, thinking part of our brain, found just behind our forehead (see figure 1). According to Dr. Bruce Perry, an expert on children and trauma and author of the book *The Boy Who Was Raised as a Dog*, we are also functioning at our optimal mental capacity, and from here we can make decisions to the best of our ability.

When we shift into a yellow-light state, we are no longer in a state of calm. This is a state of dysregulation that deserves our attention, much like a flashing yellow light on a traffic signal requires our attention. We need to proceed with caution because we are no longer in a calm, regulated state. Our thinking has shifted back toward the center part of our brain, into a more emotional place. When we are in this emotional place, we are no longer rational, as any mother of a toddler can attest. Operating from this emotional part of the brain is the equivalent of dropping about 25 IQ points! Trying to reason with someone when we or they are in a yellow-light state is generally counterproductive. Instead of speeding up when we see a yellow light, the best course of action (in a car and in life) is to slow down.

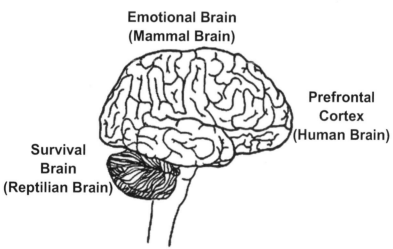

Figure 1: The Brain.

If we become more dysregulated, our thinking moves into the survival part of the brain, which is located near the base of the skull. This is a red-light state. There is literally no reasoning with someone who is in survival state. This state triggers our "fight, flight, or freeze" response, which is meant to protect us in dangerous, life-threatening situations, such as when we see a bear. Survival overrides the conscious, rational, thinking brain in favor of the part that can take immediate life-saving measures. (Indeed, there is almost no activity in the rational part of the brain when the survival brain has been activated.) We are no longer calm, and we are certainly not rational. In fact, Perry suggests that when we are in the survival state of being, we are operating at 50 points below the IQ we have in the green-light state. We are mobilized for survival, and energy is sent to our extremities so that we can fight, run away, or freeze. The energy itself isn't bad; however, we do need to learn how to move through this energy without hurting anyone or hurting ourselves until we can return to a state of calm.

Here is an example of regulation and dysregulation in action. Our family was spending the weekend with my husband's parents on their sailboat. We arrived at a little island to hunt for shells and needed to ride on a shuttle wagon that took visitors across the island to the beach. The shuttle wasn't there when we arrived, so we decided to walk across the island because it was less than one mile to the beach from the dock. My youngest, who was five years old at the time, had a very big meltdown because we had changed our plans. He went from a green-light state (excited, yet regulated) to a yellow light when we suggested not taking the shuttle, then on to a red light, in which he became completely overwhelmed, dissolving into a puddle on the sandy road.

Ideally, we would recognize the yellow-light state and create an opportunity for our child to express what is happening, or we might simply slow down in the same way we might for a flashing yellow light. When a child is in a yellow-light brain state, he needs nurturing and connection rather than rational explanations and discussions. When we can connect with our child in a yellow-light state, many times we can avoid the red-light state. Avoiding the red light is not about avoiding conflict or difficult situations for ourselves or our children, but rather helping to create patterns of being that enable everyone to return to a state of calm.

I realized my son was dysregulated, unable to calm himself down in that moment, and that meant that he needed help to regulate himself. And to regulate, he needed connection with someone who cared about him. Just this simple shift in my thinking helped me to be present with him instead of judging his behavior as wrong, as I would have done in the past. My understanding his situation didn't mean that we were going to do what he wanted to do, but it did mean that I was going to respect his feelings. We didn't turn around and go back to wait for the shuttle wagon, even though that was what he was saying he wanted to do. Instead, I got down on the ground next to him and spoke to him softly. I told him that I knew he wanted to ride on the shuttle and it was hard when things didn't go the way he thought they would go. I repeated this over and over again, calmly and patiently, yet feeling his frustration with him. More important than the words was the tone of voice I used. My words simply reflected my own understanding of such frustrations from my own life, along with my emotional connection to him. I knew he was going to express his feelings (move through the energy that was coming up for him), return to a place of calm, and then be able to go on with us to the beach. He was also going to learn that I was there for him and that I trusted that he would be able to handle this situation with my support.

Within a few minutes, he had returned to a near green-light state. He was relatively calm and ready to continue across the island, and we did so by making a game out of moving across the sand path, pretending to be animals that moved in different ways. This game also helped him to move through the rest of the energy that had just come up for him. In the past, his dysregulat-ed state might have lasted for twenty or thirty minutes, and he probably would have continued struggling with every change for the rest of the day. But because he felt heard and supported in his feelings, and he moved through the energy that came up for him, he was able to arrive at the beach a few minutes after the others and had a wonderful time exploring and collecting shells. As a side note, in the past, when I didn't know that he would move through the feelings and then calm down, I was often upset right along with him, feeling totally out of control and most likely in a red-light state myself. I experienced my own upset, in part, because, when I was growing up, I did not have the experience of moving all the way through my own feelings and back into regulation. As an adult, once I'd had my own supported experi-ences of moving through my own feelings, I was more able to support my boys' expression of feelings much more often.

We can allow the energy of our children's emotional upsets to move through us without it overtaking us, but allowing our child's emotional expression may be a new idea if, in the past, we haven't experienced moving through our own feelings. (For more about exploring emotional expression, see chapter seven.)

Communication and Connection

We live in an extremely behavior-focused society. From the moment our babies are born, others are asking us about our baby's behaviors and making judgments about whether the baby is good or bad based upon how much the baby inconveniences us as parents. But babies' behaviors are really just their way of communicating their internal state. The baby some parents may label as bad another parent would label as needing more help to adjust to the world. Do you *feel* the difference? The words we use to describe our children can help create connection or disconnec-tion right from the start.

Most parenting advice focuses on getting the baby to fit into our lives rather than taking into account what the baby needs for optimal development beyond the obvious physical needs for food and rest. When we seek only to make a behavior stop, we miss the communication and sometimes even the opportunity for our children to develop to their fullest potential.

Take the example of a child who is waking at night. One of the most frequently asked questions from the moment a child is born is, "How is the baby sleeping?" and it seems that babies are rated on their circadian rhythms and how the parents answer that question. Most advice concerning sleeping is concerned only with what the parent can do to make the baby sleep, to teach the baby to self-soothe so that she is less inconvenient for the parents. But do we stop and ask why the baby is waking up in the first place? Is the baby hungry? Does he need someone to hold him? Is she scared? Was he premature and needs extra help adjusting to the world, especially when he was in the NICU and separated from his parents while interventions were being done? What happened during the birth of the baby? Is she telling her birth story through her night waking? Is she working to communicate her story through her sounds and body movements during the night? (For more information on exploring the origins of a sleep challenge, check out the Consciously Parenting Project's audio series with Ray Castellino and Mary Jackson of aboutconnections.com. See consciouslyparenting.com/sleep.)

And what about the next layers of questions: What happens if we don't meet this need? Does it really matter? Most parenting advice usually says that it doesn't. The research shows it does. Meeting the baby's need matters a lot.

Parents who become focused on behavior when their children are young continue to focus on behavior and not their relationship with their children. As the children grow, the disconnection grows. Really alert parents may notice something isn't right early on, but not know what to do about it. Other times, parents realize that they don't have a relationship with their children when the children are preteens or teens (though sometimes much earlier) and begin acting out very loudly. By this time, the behaviors are much bigger and more problematic. The parents are more scared, and there is clearly more risk involved. (The situation isn't hopeless, but it is more challenging to repair relationships at this point than to focus on creating a healthy relationship from the start and repairing disconnections as they happen.) In contrast, the parents with a strong relationship with their children don't typically have the same problems. And those committed to making changes early on (elementary-school age or earlier is preferable) fare much better than those who wait.

Now that I'm not in the middle of the boot-throwing situation, I can see how much I wasn't able to just listen to my son and be with him long before he got to the point of throwing the boot. My own pain and isolation got in the way of our communication and kept me from seeing where he was in that moment: in need of love and connection. His behavior became my wake-up call, prompting me to step forward, reconnect with my own inner guidance system, and find a solution. Ironically, that solution wasn't actually a solution, or doing something at all, but rather about just being in the present moment with my son.

Our children communicate with us even before they are born. This communication and, more importantly, positive interaction with a committed caregiver are essential for their optimal development. As we shall see, it is the relationship that makes the difference, and our interpretation of our children's behaviors affects the way we look at the relationship. In Book III, we'll take a more in-depth look at behaviors of various developmental stages, from infancy to teens and beyond.

Questions to Ponder

- What do you look like when you're in a green-light state? What does it feel like in your body?

- What does your child look like in a green-light state? How do you know it is green?

- What do you look like in a yellow-light state? What does it feel like in your body?

- What happens to alert you to your child entering a yellow-light state? What are the early warning signs that a light change is happening?

- What do you look like in a red-light state? What might someone else observe?

- What does your child look like in a red-light state? Is it similar to what you might look like, or is it different? Does your child have a behavior you're particularly concerned about? Have you ever considered that it might be communicating part of his or her story? Does it give you hope to consider that idea, or does it feel scary for you to contemplate it?

Stoplight Brain States

Green Light	Yellow Light	Red Light
Regulated	Dysregulated; emotionally off balance	Operating from the survival brain
Operating from the cognitive, thinking brain	Operating from the emotional brain	Completely dysregulated; in survival mode
Full thinking capacity for the child's age; age-appropriate logic and conversations possible	Child's thinking capacity and reasoning ability impaired; loss of about 25 IQ points from potential until state of calm returns.	Child's thinking capacity completely impaired; loss of about 50 IQ points from potential until state of calm returns.
Attributes: Sharing Loving Peaceful Helpful Cooperative	Attributes: Refusal to help or cooperate Lack of participation Disengaged Somewhat emotional	Attributes: Fighting Taking flight (running away) Freezing (shutting down) Not able to hear individual words, but responding only to tone of voice
What the child needs: nothing, because the child's needs for loving connection are met.	*What the child needs:* nurturing and support from an adult to hold the space for feelings in connection and to return to calm.	*What the child needs:* Someone who can hear and understand the intensity of the feelings the child is experiencing. There must be connection to the child's intensity, even if that intensity doesn't make sense on a rational, intellectual level.

Green Light	Yellow Light	Red Light
		Intense energy is mobilized in this red-light state, and the child needs someone to move through the energy with him or her.
What a parent needs to do: embrace the moment.	*What a parent needs to do:* Slow everything down. Give short explanations, use few words, hold the child or stand nearby, breathe and focus on feelings. Doing any and all of these things helps child return to a calm state and reconnect with him- or herself and others. This can be a critical time for reconnecting in relationship, because both the parent and child can connect while in their emotional brains. ("I see you and understand that you're feeling sad right now. I'm feeling sad, too.") Parents don't need to *do* much, but just need to *be* with the child. Embrace the opportunity to connect!	*What a parent needs to do:* Stop the chatter and explanations. Stop trying to make the child something he or she isn't in this moment. Connect with the intensity of the upset and allow the energy to move through both of you by doing together a physical activity that requires lots of energy—running, dancing, jumping on a trampoline, hitting a cushion or large pillow, even holding very still. Have the intellectual conversation about what happened later. Note: staying artificially calm in the midst of a child's great emotional upset often leads to disconnection instead of connection. You'll know you're not connected if your child's behaviors become much more intense.

Chapter Three

Only the Relationship Matters

Principle 2: The parent-child relationship is more important than any behavioral intervention, consequence, or punishment.

"Don't touch that. I said, *don't touch that!*"

I was at Target, and I could hear a dad several aisles over trying to negotiate his way through the Easter-candy aisle with his young daughter. I immediately had empathy for him. It was late at night, and there was lots of candy about.

"Get over here right now! Get over here, or you're going to get a spanking!"

This conversation was going on loudly, and I stopped my own shopping, wondering how it would end.

"Melissa! I said not to touch that. Get over here or I'm going to spank you and strap you in the cart! Get over here, now! One. Two. Three."

I heard the shouts of a little girl, probably no more than three-years old. *"No!* I do it!"

"OK, then. Do it!"

Sound familiar?

Sounds like my house when my oldest son was about four. The only parenting tools I really had were taking something away, giving him a time-out, or using other threats. After all, he was the kid, and I was the parent. He should just do as I say, right?

We have learned over and over again in our society that behaviors are more important than anything else. Our schedule is more important than our relationship. Making our child do as we say, when we say it, becomes the goal. What we need to get done and getting our children to do what we tell them to do become more important than anything else. However, when we put the relationship first, we can set loving limits for our children that still respect our children's needs as well as our own needs. When we put behaviors, interventions, consequences, and punishments first, we are communicating that the behavior is more important than the child, and that unspoken message creates disconnection.

Old Situations, New Responses

I was speaking with a parent named Misti, and she described this situation with her three-year-old:

Rachel has been having temper tantrums every
day—probably ten times a day lately. And it
seems like it is never really anything huge that
sets her off. Tonight we were heading upstairs to
go to bed, and she refused to go. I was tired, and
I didn't have time to deal with it. She needed to
go upstairs right now because it was time for her
to get ready for bed. So I picked her up and
headed up the stairs with her kicking and
screaming at me. What else could I have done?

Rachel was clearly overwhelmed, and Misti didn't understand
why. We can't blame Misti for wanting to get her daughter to bed
and for being tired after a long day filled with temper tantrums.
Rachel probably was tired and needed to be put to bed. *But she
also needed to have her feelings about it, and she needed her
mom to "get" her.* Misti could have started up for bed earlier,
before she and Rachel were totally exhausted, so that she could
have put her relationship with her daughter first and thus
connected with Rachel to help her daughter regulate her feelings.
A calm, regulated child will go to sleep much more easily than
one who is still totally dysregulated and distressed, so it is
definitely worth the time and effort it would take Misti to
connect with Rachel and help her regulate her feelings.

Interestingly, when I next spoke to Misti, she shared
with me that when she started putting the relationship first by
stopping to acknowledge her daughter, focusing on staying
emotionally present, and recognizing Rachel's feelings were her
feelings and that she had a right to them in that moment, there
was almost an instant decrease in the temper tantrums. The ones
her daughter did have were longer at first, as I'd told her they
would be, but then things seemed to go a bit easier.

Misti also said that the hardest part was not knowing
why her daughter was so upset. I shared with her that being a
three-year-old was probably reason enough all by itself. Rachel

did have several traumatic and overwhelming events as a part of her story, and I pointed out that all the temper tantrums Misti described occurred at transition times. Difficulty with transitions is very common for young children. It is also common for older children with unfinished trauma as a part of their story, because they are more prone to having times where they are emotionally younger than their chronological age. (See Book III for a more detailed look at handling transitions with young children.)

Let's turn to that ever-so-common situation of a child who won't stay in bed at night. We parents normally are told to create consequences for when the child gets out of bed, such as loss of privileges, so that the child will learn not to get out of bed. This advice is based on the old thinking that if we're happy to see our child out of bed or if we offer them what they need, the child will continue to do it over and over again. In other words, we reinforce the "bad" behavior by giving the child a "positive" response to it. The only way to make the behavior stop, according to this theory, is to punish the behavior.

When we're looking at this situation with our new awareness, we might consider that the child needs something other than another cup of water or a snack. Perhaps the child is hungry or thirsty, but what if the child really needs emotional connection? What if the child is scared? A consequence doesn't make that need go away, does it?

When I suggest to parents that they work to connect with their child as much as possible throughout the day so that the child isn't going to bed still feeling a big need for connection, bedtime goes much more smoothly for most parents. *When the need is met, the behavior goes away without punishment.* Many parents, whether they are stay-at-home parents or not, don't realize how little time they are actually spending in connection with each child during the day. In fact, surveys have shown that stay-at-home parents spend only slightly higher number of minutes exclusively interacting with their children than parents who work outside the home do. The average for both was only about fifteen minutes per day. We may physically be in the same place with our children, but we are not necessarily interacting with one another in an emotionally connected way.

On another deeper level, when a child has experienced something overwhelming in his or her life, it is common that this pain comes out at bedtime (or other transitions points during the daytime). Ray Castellino and Mary Jackson take a closer look at how parents can support their children by looking deeper and create healing in the family in the audio series we recorded together. (See consciouslyparenting.com/LPBC.)

I once worked with another parent, a single mom named Mari, who often came home late from work very tired and needed her eight-year-old daughter, Sofi, to help out with the housework. Mari was very focused on doing what needed to be done to keep the house running and to get both of them ready to go the next day, and she was getting very frustrated with Sofi because the girl didn't want to get right down to business and put away the clean clothes. (What self-respecting eight-year-old would?) Mari tried punishments, she tried offering rewards, but nothing seemed to work.

I suggested that Sofi was really needing connection with Mari after they'd been apart all day and Mari should try spending just ten or fifteen minutes paying attention to her daughter before asking her to do anything. Just sit together or do something that she would like to do, I told her. Mari was a bit reluctant at first, since they had very little time in the evening and so much to do, but she was willing to try anything at that point.

When I spoke to Mari next, she excitedly shared that everything was going much more smoothly. Initially, she had found it very difficult to stop thinking about the long list of things that needed to be done, but she worked hard to stay focused on the most important job she had to do after work—connecting with her daughter. Mari reported that, amazingly, all the work was getting done, and it had actually become fun. She and Sofi were working together, and the jobs were taking less than half the time that they had been taking. Gone were the disconnection and the need to use consequences to get her daughter to comply with her orders. When Mari focused on the relationship, the problem practically dissolved. She was ecstatic.

Connection Instead of Consequences

Many parents get very wrapped up in delivering the appropriate consequence. One parenting "expert" has suggested that parents make a list of their children's bothersome behaviors and the appropriate consequences and post the list on the refrigerator, so that the parent will know what consequence to give out when the child misbehaves. This seems like a good idea on the surface. "Everyone knows what to expect" is definitely an argument for this method. But it is not about connection, relationship, or looking at the unique circumstances or the individual person in front of us. It isn't looking below the surface of someone's actions to create understanding. It is simply a method of trying to make a behavior that we don't like go away, and chances are it won't work in the way we hope it will. Most parents know this deep down. With this method, if the child does what we tell them to do, it isn't because they have learned intrinsically that the behavior is good or bad, but rather that bad things will happen if they don't do what we say. The bottom line is that parenting techniques that use threats and coercion are really threatening the child's core need of love and attention (what a child needs to survive) to gain temporary compliance. A compliant child is very different than a child who is connected in relationship to you and wants to please you and do what you ask out of mutual respect.

Even cellular biology tells us that we are designed to be in relationship. According to Bruce Lipton, in his book *Biology of Belief*, cells on a petri dish, when separated, will move back together to communicate with one another. In order to grow optimally, our brains need interactions with significant others who care about us deeply. Without human contact in close proximity and emotional connection in our early years, we will die. Without continued contact, connection, and acceptance of loving individuals in our life, we may survive, but not thrive or grow to our potential. Our energy will be going toward surviving and holding feelings down, forcing ourselves to express them in other more "acceptable" ways, all so that we will, hopefully, be accepted.

Or if we cannot hold back the feelings, we may warrant a diagnosis and medication. Why do we have such an epidemic of children with attention-deficit disorder (ADD), attention-deficit/hyperactivity disorder (ADHD), and myriad other labels? Ultimately, at the root of the vast majority of these diagnoses, are trauma and relationships that are unable to meet the children's connection needs. Eventually, the parents reach out for help and are handed a diagnostic label for the child and a prescription that will supposedly help the child to cope (and help the parents cope with the child's behavior). The label and the drug can't fix the core trauma or disconnection, though, even if they do mask the symptoms temporarily.

Relationship, not medication, is the missing link. But most parents don't understand that, nor do they know how to connect with their children to help them through the symptoms and understand what they are attempting to communicate through their behaviors. It isn't that parents are bad or lazy; they simply don't know any other way. Finding alternative answers that will make a difference in the child's life long term requires a new level of awareness.

Not having a punishment lined up for each behavioral challenge doesn't mean that there aren't any limits set for our children. In fact, limits are an essential part of parenting consciously.

One father shared a story about setting a limit without using a consequence or a punishment. Keith took his son, Josh, to the store. Josh was recently diagnosed with food allergies, and

Keith knew that not being allowed to have many of the foods on the store shelves is difficult for Josh. When they reached the peanut butter aisle, Josh started to melt down because he wanted peanut butter, which was his favorite food until his allergy was discovered. Josh cried and yelled loudly, and many other shoppers stopped to watch.

Although Keith felt the urge to either grab Josh and run out of the store or yell at him to stop, he was able to regulate his own feelings of shame and anger that came up because of Josh's behavior; he did so by focusing on his breathing and thinking about how difficult this situation must be for Josh. After taking in the whole scene to figure out what Josh needed in this moment, he realized that Josh didn't actually need peanut butter. Josh was really feeling angry about the seemingly unfair limit. Keith remembered times in his life when something seemed really unfair, so he could relate to Josh's feelings and approach Josh with compassion.

He leaned over to Josh and said, "I know this is really hard and you really wish you could have peanut butter. I need to keep you safe and that means that you can't have peanut butter right now. I'm really sorry." He put his arms around Josh to comfort him, and Josh climbed onto his dad's lap. It took a few minutes for Josh to settle, stop crying, and start to use words again. Then, tears still in his eyes, he asked his dad if there was something else he could have instead of peanut butter to have on a sandwich. Together, they began to explore the choices in the store aisle and found sunflower butter, an acceptable alternative.

In this situation, Keith and Josh maintained their connection through the upsetting tantrum, and Dad maintained the limit he needed to set to keep Josh safe. As a side note, there can still be a good connection between Keith and Josh even if Keith hadn't handled this situation as well as he did. As long as there is the emotional space in the relationship for reconnection—space for Keith to come back to Josh and say that he hadn't handled it well and was sorry (bonding behaviors) or for Josh to come to

Keith and reconnect after his tantrum (attachment behaviors)—the relationship can be healthy and secure. In fact, I read recently that the most attuned parents only catch about 30 percent of their child's cues, which means that the "best" parents are missing 70 percent!

Consciously parenting isn't about having the perfect response to every situation, but maintaining a parenting relationship that is open for reconnection and repair. Parents do have to take responsibility for their own stories and work to not simply repeat the unhealthy patterns they grew up with, but they certainly don't have to be perfect. (Phew!)

Honoring the Relationship Respects Everyone's Needs

So what about that dad in Target? What could he have done differently to connect with his young daughter in relationship instead of focusing on the girl's behavior?

Before they even went into the store, Dad might have had said something like, "Last time we were in Target, I think it was too overwhelming for you. I'm going to make some different choices that will feel better for everyone. I'm going to put you right up here, in the cart seat, where we can talk. We'll spend time together and enjoy our trip!"

If Dad didn't talk to his daughter in advance and found himself in the situation in the Easter-candy aisle, he might have handled it by first allowing himself to slow down (noticing the yellow light for either himself or his daughter) and kneeling to meet Melissa at eye level before speaking. Then he could connect with her by saying something such as, "Melissa, I think this aisle is much too overwhelming for you. Come and sit in the cart so we can spend time together. I love you very much, and it is my job to keep you safe. Would you like to hold your toy to give your hands something to do? Would you like to climb up while I hold the cart, or do you want me to help you get into your seat?"

Dad's need is for Melissa to stay safe and to have a peaceful visit to the store. Perhaps Melissa's need is to explore and stay connected to Dad. How could Melissa stay safe *and* still explore? One strategy might be for Melissa to sit in the cart so she's closer to eye level. Dad could pay attention to what Melissa seems interested in and hand her some safe, appropriate objects to explore as they walk through the store. He might talk to her as they shop, sharing what he sees or what they're going to do next. The solutions are numerous when we begin to focus on needs of the relationship rather than the behavior of the child.

There are no threats involved in the relationship-focused solutions. Dad would realize that this situation is too much for his daughter, so he would create safety for her. He would remain connected to himself and connected in relationship to his daughter without giving up, without threats, without consequences. He would finish his shopping as quickly as possible and leave the store. Next time he goes, he would consider going to the store earlier, before she's too tired, and he would be proactive and put her in the cart from the beginning. He wouldn't say that because she was bad last time they went to Target, she has to sit in the cart this time around. Instead, he would focus on the relationship and emphasize his need to keep her safe, giving her every opportunity to stay within the boundaries while creating a trip to Target that is enjoyable for both him and her.

By putting the relationship first, by focusing on the needs of their child and on their own needs, parents can set limits and still stay connected with their child. In the case of the Target dad and his daughter, Dad would not be permitting his daughter to run around the store, but the experience would become positive for both of them. Doesn't that experience feel totally different than the original situation?

Something that has helped me tremendously in my journey as a parent is remembering that I am doing the best I can in any given moment—and so is my child. He wants to connect with me. If he's not behaving as I hope he would, his behavior is letting me know that something isn't right in his world, something isn't right in my world, and/or something isn't right in our connection. When I'm not behaving appropriately, I don't need a consequence. Sometimes I need boundaries. Sometimes I need support. But I always need connection with somebody, and so do our children.

Because, from the time we were small children, we are programmed to look at behaviors and consequences, it takes mindfulness and lots of practice to start seeing situations differently. But when we start seeing the possibility of a different outcome, we can start finding solutions that result in connection and a stronger relationship with our children.

Questions to Ponder

- What are your children's most concerning behaviors? Choose one and write about it.

- What do you normally do when your child behaves this way?

- When did the behavior start? What was happening in your life? What was happening in your child's life?

- Could it be possible that your child is trying to communicate a need through this behavior? What would it mean if your child were communicating something important to you, and you could understand it?

- What would it take for you to shift to a place of compassion when your child expresses a "negative" behavior?

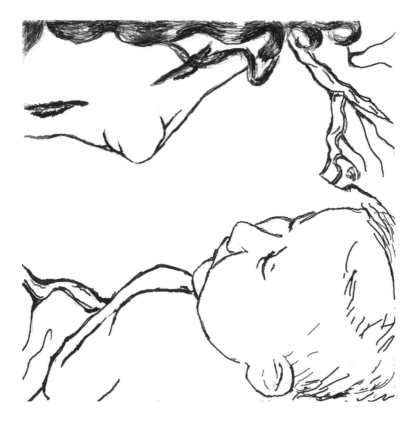

Chapter Four

Neuroscience and the Importance of Attachment

Principle 3: Children unfold neurosequentially, and quality, connected relationships allow for the unfolding. A need met will go away; a need unmet is here to stay.

Neurosequential is a big word, but it simply means that the brain develops in a specific order, both in utero and after birth. When the baby's brain is first forming, it develops from the base of the brain (the least complex part) upward to the top front, or the prefrontal cortex (the most complex part). The base of the brain, the so-called primitive brain, is responsible for regulating respiration, body functions, and fight, flight, or freeze responses— in other words, basic survival. The emotional center, or the limbic system, develops next, followed by the cognitive prefrontal cortex, or "thinking" brain. After a child is born, the same order of development repeats as each brain system matures and learns from the environment around itself.

Mothers have known for eons that the cry of a baby demands attention; when left to their own innate devices, most mothers will comfort a crying baby, regardless of whether or not the baby is even hers. Crying is babies' primary form of communication with the world, allowing them to let their caregiver know that they are tired, wet, hungry, needing to be held, or otherwise needing attention. The basic needs of infants are not really a surprise: They need to be held. They need responsive caregiving. They need emotionally mature and present caregivers who are able to meet those early needs. They need someone who will keep them safe from harm. They need someone who can model positive ways of interacting with the world and demonstrate those ways over and over again. It is through these responsive relationships that babies grow and develop optimally. Neuroscience is discovering that this dance between mother and baby, and later between other caregivers and young child, is essential to optimal brain development and to preventing later dysfunction in all areas of life. The preconception environment and the stress levels a woman experiences during pregnancy, as well as the care a child receives during her first three to five years of life, influence the structure of the developing brain and lay down the neurological wiring for later functioning.

Research has shown that in our early years we need consistent, loving care from a specific person who is attuned to our needs. For example, we need to be held frequently, because in our early years, we learn best through physical touch (and how our caregiver feels when he or she is close to us) rather than any words someone says. The sense of safety allows us to focus on growing in all domains, rather than simply on survival.

Children whose basic early needs were not met are more likely to be stuck in a survival-mode pattern, where their lower brain areas dominate their behaviors. This means that they are not in a conscious, thinking place, but rather are living in a state of fear or being overwhelmed. They tend to be easily reactive and not easily soothed. They can be shut down (hypoaroused) or overly reactive (hyperaroused).

Unfortunately, children in orphanages, particularly in Eastern European group homes, have taught us much about what happens when those basic needs are not met during the first three years of life. Some of these children have difficulty connecting with others in meaningful ways and actually seem to prefer solitude. Their behaviors may seem odd to outside observers, or the children may seem "normal" to everyone except those who are caring for them. The early needs of these children were not met, and these needs did not go away. When a child doesn't connect with a caring person who meets her needs early in life, she learns that her needs aren't going to be met in a relationship. She learns to cope with her own needs the best she can, many times through solitude, even though it remains that her deepest need is to connect deeply with someone who really cares. It takes dedication and the right interventions to help these children develop anywhere close to their potential.

These children's situations are extreme, but the same is true for all of us. Basic early needs do not simply go away when we grow older. These early patterns of relationship, for better or for worse, create the relationship patterns we follow through the course of our lives. If our own basic needs were not met when we were children, it becomes very difficult for us to meet them in our own children. For example, if our own parents followed the standard parenting advice of generations past, which encouraged parents to let babies cry rather than holding them as needed for fear of spoiling them, we have templates within our brain telling us to make the same decisions. When we weren't comforted when we were upset, we are less likely to comfort our own child when they are in a similar situation. We may listen to our child scream and not feel anything about it. Conversely, we may be aware of our early experiences and our feelings about our early care and not allow our child to cry for a single minute. If our early experiences were less than optimal, we may need more support to parent optimally than parents who had more nurturing early childhood experiences.

Patterns of Relationship: Attachment

The basis for our understanding of relationships and optimal child development is *attachment theory*, which was originally developed in the 1950s by John Bowlby, when he observed children who had been left in hospitals without a parent. In England at the time, it was thought that young children hospitalized for illness would do better without the parents visiting the hospital and bringing outside germs to the sick child. So children were usually left on their own, with no visits from or other contact with their parents, for weeks or months. Bowlby documented, on camera, the stages of grief these children went through at the loss of their parents. Essentially, they lost the person or people who meant the most to them and who could help them deal with the stress of the illness for which they were being hospitalized. As a result, they became depressed and despondent. Healthy development cannot occur if a child is in a survival state, without anyone to help modulate the stresses of life.

Bowlby said that all relationships are built on the foundation of our past relationship experiences, primarily those relationships we had with our caregivers in the first three years of our lives.

Bowlby's research was the first to look at the importance of special human relationships called *attachment relationships*: the relationships we have in our earliest years and through which our brains are actually organized. Even though we don't remember these relationships, the care we received or didn't receive, along with how our parents (or other caregivers) felt about our care, our needs, and about us specifically, has a powerful influence over who we become as adults. The relationships we have in our earliest lives also establish the way that we will look at all relationships throughout our lives, for better or worse. Our earliest relationships—those that happen before we are three years old—strongly influence who we are, what we struggle with in our lives on all levels, and what kind of parents we become.

This is great news if our parents themselves were treated with unconditional love and respect, were wanted and appreciated, and had their feelings valued as young children. However, if our parents weren't treated this way, they most likely repeated the same patterns when they became parents unless they made a conscious effort to change. How our parents *felt* about taking care of us was just as important as how they cared for us and the decisions they made about our care. Most of us are not even aware of the patterns that we carry from our earliest experiences, so we might be destined to repeat the same patterns without even knowing why. But we can change the patterns once we become more aware of them.

Basically, we need other people to survive and thrive, regardless of our age. Daniel J. Siegel, psychiatrist, scientist, educator, and leader in the field of mental health, discusses the social nature of our brains and refutes the antiquated view of the "single skull theory," which says our mind is contained only within our own body. We are fiercely social creatures, and our brains actually interact with one another and develop through this healthy interdependence. Infants are born without sufficient regulatory ability, and they need a responsive caregiver who can help them learn to return themselves to a state of calm. In fact, it is through their relationship with us as parents that our babies learn to connect with themselves. When we respond to our little one's hungry cry, our baby learns to know when she is hungry. Until someone repeatedly responds to those hunger cues, our babies do not differentiate one feeling of discomfort from another. If a parent responds to a baby's cries of discomfort by feeding them food instead of emotional nourishment, the child may grow up confusing their physical and emotional needs. We learn who we are and what we need by sharing those experiences with others from the time we are very small. There is no *I*, only *we*, for we are all shaped by one another.

Some people believe that because we can't consciously remember our lives before the age of three or later, anything that happens to us at that time has no effect on us. But brain science says differently. The sequential way the brain develops explains why we usually can't remember our earliest lives: at that age, the hippocampus, the part of our brain that stores conscious memories, is not yet developed. But the amygdala, in concert with our implicit memory system, is developed and records in our unconscious every detail of everything that happens to us. "Early childhood traumas can disturb the mental and behavioural functions of adults by mechanisms that they cannot access consciously," writes Bruno Dubuc of the Canadian Institutes of Health Research (Institute of Neurosciences, Mental Health and Addiction) in the Web-based presentation "The Brain from Top to Bottom." Even though we cannot consciously recall the care we received as infants—good or bad—our unconscious mind is reminded of it through sensory cues (sights, sounds, smells, feelings, and touch), and how we behave in response to those cues shows us what we experienced.

Parenting has a unique way of bringing up those situations from our own past that were less than optimal and are in need of healing. You may look back on your childhood and think that things were just great, but looking at the optimal experiences described in Book II may help you identify difficult areas or incidents that, in the past, you weren't identifying as stressful. The good news is that the brain is capable of changing throughout our lives, so it is no longer thought that someone with poor early experiences is doomed to a poor outcome. (Of course, changing the brain isn't instantaneous and requires commitment and dedication, so it is best if we provide our own children with the best possible beginnings.)

Attachment and Bonding: A Two-Way Street

Little Caroline came into the world right at forty weeks, but her home birth was anything but peaceful for Mom or baby. Her mom, Kate, and Caroline were both traumatized physically and emotionally during the birth and were in no way ready to connect with one another. Caroline's pediatrician was concerned about her breathing, and she was taken to the NICU for several days. Once she came home, she screamed inconsolably for most of the day, every day. Kate and her partner, Dan, were understandably exhausted.

Unfortunately, this family's story isn't unique. Kate and Dan were both eager to bond with their baby, but the post-birth separation and then sheer exhaustion left them unable to connect in the way they wanted. When we don't understand our child's communication with us and that they're trying to show us their story through their cries, their body movements, and their behavior patterns, we often feel at a loss for how to connect with them. In Book II, we'll be taking a closer look at how to change disconnection after a difficult beginning, even if it is years later.

It takes both attachment, which refers to the baby's attempts to connect with the parents, as well as bonding, the parents' attempts to connect with the baby, to create a secure attachment. Unrepaired disconnections can affect the course of the relationship. If Caroline and Kate had stayed in the place of disconnection (Caroline screaming, and Kate feeling like she was an ineffective mother because she couldn't calm her baby), they probably would have survived, but not connected deeply in the way they needed to.

Bonding and attachment is the process of a baby and parent falling in love with each other and each doing his or her part to connect, knowing that there are going to be bumpy roads and missed connections along the way. We don't have to connect perfectly (an impossibility), but we need to work to see our children's perspective and attempts to connect with us, even if their attempts come at us in a way that we may not understand at first, like Caroline's screaming. Once Caroline's parents understood what she was communicating, they were able to connect, to bond, to attach.

To learn more about what our children are showing us in their early months and years, see Book II, "Creating Connection."

Questions to Ponder

- What do you want for your kids when they grow up? Who do you want them to become? What defines success or happiness in your mind?

- What are your fears for your children? Where did those fears come from?

- What was your childhood like? Do you have positive early memories?

- What do you want your child to remember about you from his or her childhood? What is your child likely to remember?

What Is Attachment?
What Is Bonding?

- Attachment is the forming of a special, enduring "emotional" relationship between a child and a primary caregiver (in childhood, this is usually the mother).

- Attachment is how the child's behaviors create a connected relationship with the caregiver.

- Bonding is how the caregiver's behaviors create a connected relationship with the child.

- Attachment relationships involve comfort, soothing, and pleasure (think rocking, nursing, holding, joy).

- The child becomes distressed at the loss (or the threat of the loss) of the caregiver.

- Safety for both child and the caregiver is found in this relationship.

- Both bonding and attachment are required to create a connected relationship.

Chapter Five

How Our Needs Influence
Our Children's Behaviors

Principle 4: Behaviors occur on a continuum. Behaviors in children (and parents, too) correlate to the parent's own neurodevelopment and attachment status.

The more we had our early needs met, the more our own children will develop optimally. The more difficulty our parents had meeting our needs when we were young children, or the more difficulty they had navigating discipline with us, the more difficulty we are going to have parenting our own children.

If we did not receive unconditional love and acceptance from our parents, it is nearly impossible for us to give these to our own children, unless we have since had a relationship with someone who was able to give those things to us and we were able to receive them. There are countless stories of children and adults who had one person care about them—whether it was a coach, a teacher, a foster parent, or someone else in the community who took an interest in the person's life—and this one caring person made all the difference. For us as adults, it takes one good relationship with what Greg Baer, author of the book *Real Love*, calls a "Wise Friend." This is someone who can help you see things as they actually are and who can love you unconditionally while you connect with your own inner guidance (my words).

Attachment research in more recent years has found very strong correlations between what is called **infant attachment status** and **adult attachment status**. The patterns children have in their earliest years have been measured through clinical observations, and when the same children are tested again as adults, there is a strong likelihood that they will exhibit the same attachment status and patterns of relationship as when they were young children. The quality of relationships in our first year of life creates patterns that are easily observable (by trained observers), and these patterns can predict our childhood ability, and our later ability as an adult, to form healthy relationships—or not. *It is through these very patterns of relationship that we can further understand ourselves and how we interact in all of our relationships, including those with our children.*

Secure and Insecure Attachment

Infant attachment status is determined using a laboratory study with one-year-olds called the "Strange Situation." An infant's primary caregiver is invited to bring the child to a room the child has never been to before. The child enters with the caregiver and starts to play. A stranger then enters the room, and the child is observed to see how he responds. The caregiver then leaves the room and, a minute later, returns. The child's reaction when the caregiver returns is very telling and a big determining factor in deciding the child's attachment status. If the child comes up to the caregiver, makes eye contact, and usually also some physical contact, and then returns to play, the child is said to have a **secure attachment.** If the child has another response when the caregiver returns, the child is categorized as having an **insecure attachment** with that caregiver.

Secure attachment does not result from perfect parenting, but from good-enough parenting. Children with a secure attachment have responsive care during their early experiences with a caregiver. They are held frequently, their needs are met as they communicate those needs to the outside world, and they are treated with love and respect. This type of care should be the norm for all children, but sadly it is not. And traditional parenting advice does not help to create it.

As a child with a secure attachment grows older, her parents continue to connect and nurture the relationship, taking responsibility to repair the relationship following misunderstandings or other disconnections. As the child grows, she is able to communicate her needs openly and with respect to those around her and to reach out for support as needed. Yet she generally acts with a degree of independence because her early needs were met. (Those whose needs aren't met become superficially independent because they had no other choice.)

Let's take Ariel, for example. Because her parents wanted to get a good night's sleep, they wanted a baby who didn't need them too much and who didn't depend on Mom or Dad to put her to sleep. So when Ariel was three months old, they decided to let her cry herself to sleep so she would learn to fall asleep on her own. After more than a week of crying for as long as an hour after being put to bed, Ariel finally "learned" to fall asleep on her own. However, Ariel's mom also noticed that she seemed somewhat despondent and not her usual self during the day. Their happy baby was suddenly not happy anymore.

Ariel had no real choices for responding to her parents' decision to let her cry herself to sleep. She needed comfort and soothing, but it didn't come to her as it had in her first three months. So she *had* to become more independent and disconnect from her own basic needs. Ariel didn't become more mature or independent than other babies her age; she became more disconnected from herself and her parents than she had been. If this disconnection from her parents and from her own needs continued, she would fit the criteria for a child with an insecure attachment.

Parents Kendall and Rob were in a very similar situation. Having been given a book about teaching children to sleep through the night, they decided to try the book's advice with their son, William. After about a week of intense crying at nap times and bedtime, William started to sleep better, as the book had promised. However, Kendall noticed William didn't seem like himself. She followed her instincts and decided to bring him back into the co-sleeper in their room and respond to him at night. (A co-sleeper is a special bassinet designed to be positioned right next to the parents' bed, so one parent or the other can easily reach out and touch the child throughout the night.) After a few days of this arrangement and Kendall making an extra effort to spend lots of skin-to-skin time with William during the day, he was back to himself. He woke up during the night a bit more often, but he was clearly more content. When he was evaluated as part of an attachment study at the age of one year, he was considered to have a secure attachment with both his mother and father.

As adults, individuals with a secure attachment generally have healthy relationships in which they maintain their sense of self, and they form interdependent relationships rather than codependent relationships. (The typical example of a codependent relationship is one with a spouse that is an alcoholic and abusive, yet the other spouse stays in the relationship, enabling the first person to find his next drink because she feels it is her responsibility to do so at the expense of her own needs.) Those with a secure attachment have a coherent life story, or narrative, which means that they have made sense of their experiences and relationships. Having a secure attachment doesn't mean that there were never any struggles or challenges in their childhood (or adulthood, for that matter). It means that when those difficult experiences did happen, there were others around to offer support, and the securely attached people were able to accept the support. They were able to talk about a negative experience so that eventually they were able to reach a sense of peace and forgiveness about what happened. When they talk about the same negative experience in the present time, the memory isn't emotionally charged, and it makes sense both to the person telling the story and anyone else who is listening. Adults' levels of attachment are measured using an instrument called the Adult Attachment Interview (AAI), an interview procedure designed for use by psychologists.

Three Types of Insecure Attachment

The same Strange Situation laboratory setting that determines whether a child has a secure or insecure attachment can also determine what type of insecure attachment a child has. There are three types: avoidant, anxious, and disorganized attachment. (These areas correlate to the adult states of dismissing, preoccupied, and disoriented, as defined by the AAI.) When one-year-olds with insecure attachments are in the Strange Situation, an observer can see them do one of three things: (1) ignore the caregiver's return (avoidant), (2) cling to the caregiver when she returns (anxious), or (3) move toward and then away from the caregiver (disorganized), sometimes backing away while facing the caregiver.

A child who has an **avoidant attachment** has already learned that the caregiver is probably not going to meet his needs and that it is futile to reach out for help or support. This caregiver probably had a dismissive caregiver as his primary care provider when he was a baby. This caregiver invalidates the needs the child expresses, perhaps because his or her own needs were never met as a baby. This child's basic needs, such as for food, will be met, but most likely on a schedule determined by the caregiver rather than the needs expressed by the child. Comfort is offered when the caregiver feels it is warranted. Many children who are left to "cry it out" in order to learn to sleep may later be identified as having an avoidant attachment with their caregiver.

A child who has an **anxious attachment** with her caregiver probably receives unpredictable care; sometimes the caregiver is connected to the child and meets her needs, while other times not. When the caregiver is able to connect, the child is likely to cling because she is not sure what is going to happen next. Caregivers who are preoccupied, perhaps with something going on in their personal lives, or those caregivers whose own parents were preoccupied for one reason or another, have a much higher likelihood of being anxiously attached themselves. When they were children, their basic needs were met, though their primary caregiver probably wasn't fully emotionally present. An interesting example of an adult with anxious (or preoccupied) attachment is a mother I worked with; she felt anxious when she was around her baby, but had no idea why. When we started to dig a little further, we realized that her own mother had been anxious during her pregnancy and her daughter's infancy because her father was away at war. Although the grandmother was anxious about something that had nothing to do with her daughter, she unknowingly passed her anxiety on to the next generation—the mother I was working with.

A child with a **disorganized attachment** is at the highest risk of developing difficulties in later childhood and in adulthood. A high percentage of people with disorganized attachment in childhood have emotional disorders as they grow older. This child experiences erratic, and many times abusive, parenting. As a result, the child is drawn to the caregiver for survival, yet is met with inconsistent care, which makes the child want to withdraw to protect himself. If our parents encountered abuse when they were children, they may not abuse us, but their parenting is likely to be inconsistent. And they likely give us mixed signals about whether or not it is OK for us to communicate our needs and feelings.

Disconnection is going to be part of the journey for a caregiver who hasn't made sense of her own story. As an adult, this individual has pieces of her story that do not make sense. Most commonly, this person will get confused about the present time, because unresolved situations coming up in the present feel like situations from the past. While this confusion can happen in any of the insecure attachment states, it is likely to happen more frequently with a person with a disorganized/disoriented attachment.

One mom recently shared with me what it can look like when a part of a story that hasn't been integrated suddenly pops up in daily life.

> One night [my son] Arthur was going to read to
> me at bedtime. When I went in, I noticed that
> all his pocket money was out of the moneybox
> and on his side table. I was annoyed. I'd told
> him time and again not to leave it out, or else it
> gets lost. So I asked him to put it back in the box.
> He started doing it, but ever so slowly. And sud-
> denly I blew up at him and started telling him
> off, and I told him he had taken so long that
> there wasn't enough time to hear him read.

Then I stomped out of the room. I went down
to my bedroom to cool off. I realized almost immediately that this was such a gross overreaction
and that he had, in fact, not done anything
wrong at all. This was 100 percent about me.
I had no idea what it was about, but I stayed in
my room until I calmed down (about five to ten
minutes, I think). And then I went back in and
apologized to him for my outburst—and listened
to him read.

Overreacting to situations involving our children is the hallmark
of something that is unresolved from our past, as happened with
this mom. Upon reflection, she may have discovered that the
trigger for her was that Arthur hadn't listened to her or that he
seemed to be dragging his feet. Or perhaps it was that he wasn't
treating his money with respect or that Mom herself wasn't
feeling respected. Situations in the present may remind us
(subconsciously at first) of situations that didn't work out the
way we wanted them to when we were younger. When we become aware of them, we have the opportunity to heal from those
situations in the present moment.

The Effect of Trauma on Attachment

Trauma has a profound impact on a person's ability to attach,
particularly if the trauma occurs early in life and more so if the
trauma is a relational trauma—a trauma that occurs with someone who is supposed to love and care for this person. When a
caregiver is abusive or very inconsistent, many times it means
she hasn't become aware of the traumatic experiences in her own
past and found ways to integrate those experiences into her
personal narrative. Without the awareness and vigilance to make
the necessary changes, every day she can unknowingly act out
her old story in her parenting interactions. Early secure-

attachment relationships protect against trauma, but trauma early in life can threaten a person's ability to form attachment relationships later. The early patterns in our life can often predict our ability to recover, or not recover, from the inevitable traumas of life. The ability to reach out to others, to open up to someone else, to experience our feelings, and to express our painful experiences can keep us from developing disorders such as post-traumatic stress disorder (PTSD) with its debilitating flashbacks, night terrors, and startle responses. Children diagnosed with reactive attachment disorder (RAD) always have disrupted relationships in their early caregiving experiences.

Reactive Attachment Disorder

Reactive attachment disorder (RAD) is often diagnosed in children who, in their first few years of life, were unable to form a close relationship with a caregiver. RAD is common in adopted children, particularly those children who were in placed in foster care or orphanages where only their most basic physical needs were met. Children diagnosed with RAD often display severe behaviors as a result of these early unmet needs; they may seek connection in inappropriate ways or situations in a subconscious attempt to get those needs met. Lying, stealing, inappropriate affection with strangers, hoarding and gorging on food, rages, or shutting-down behaviors are common in children diagnosed with RAD. (See the resources section for relationship-focused treatment of reactive attachment disorder.)

Earned Secure Attachment

Earned secure attachment is a designation given to someone with an insecure attachment who integrates his or her history into a coherent narrative and works through the negative issues from the past. One way to integrate is to tell the stories of your life in connection with someone who cares for you, sharing your thoughts and feelings and staying connected to your body sensations (that feeling in the pit of your stomach, for example, as you talk about your traumatic birth or your bad day at work).

Individuals can work on their own or with a therapist or coach who is very knowledgeable about attachment issues in adults. The process needs to involve not only a cognitive component, but an emotional component as well. Cognitive-behavioral therapy may be the most researched type of therapy, but it doesn't effectively resolve attachment issues or change behaviors in the long term.

One of the best people to work on these issues with is your partner, if he or she is willing. Your partner's issues create the perfect opportunity for you to work through whatever issues you need to work through with the right support. I find most couples don't have any difficulty identifying the emotionally charged issues between them, but those issues are never about content. We can have the same fight for twenty years and not resolve it, or we can learn how to create connection and truly listen to our partner in order to heal. Many couples find attachment-focused couples coaching or counseling to be a very effective way of learning new patterns of relationship. I highly recommend Encounter-Focused Couples Therapy, developed by Hedy Schleifer, LMHC, with its lovely process of creating connection in couples through "crossing the bridge" into the world of your partner. I haven't seen anything that creates a safe space for couples more effectively than Hedy's work. (Explore *www.hedyyumi.com* for more information.)

Vicky, for example, came from parents who were abusive, belittled her, and were unable to support her feelings or her healthy growth and development. She went through many unsuccessful relationships, struggled with her health, and fell into a deep depression when she became pregnant by a man she had known only a few weeks. Despite being together only a short time, Jim and Vicky decided to try to make this relationship work for themselves and their unborn baby. The relationship was rocky at best, never really having a chance to get a strong footing before they were navigating parenthood together. Each blamed the other for everything they felt was going wrong, and neither had been able to see the other person's view of the world. They couldn't even understand why they stayed in a relationship where each of them felt unseen, unheard, and misunderstood.

What was happening? Jim and Vicky were playing out their early attachment relationship patterns with each other. Our partner can be our biggest challenge in our lives *and* our biggest opportunity for healing our early attachment patterns. It took many months, but working together Jim and Vicky were able to connect with one another deeply, to hear each other's fears and concerns, and move forward in their relationship. When they were able to connect deeply with one another, they healed very old patterns. As a result of this deep healing work, Vicky changed her attachment status from insecure to earned secure—and changed the course of her life. It is never too late or too much to heal when there is determination and the right support. (See *www.consciouslyparentingbook.com* for a list of suggested books, videos, and individuals who offer this kind of support for our partnerships.)

A Real-Life Example of Insecure Attachment

So what does an insecure attachment look like in a family? What does it really mean? Here's an example based upon a client

I worked with, though names and details have been changed to protect the confidentiality of this family.

Janet looked forward to becoming a mother and couldn't wait to have a baby of her own. After years of infertility, she finally was able to have a baby. Within a few months, she found herself overwhelmed with caring for this tiny baby, who seemed to need so much of her. Within a few more months, she developed an illness and had to hire someone to help care for her baby. Before the baby was a year old, she learned that she was expecting again. When the second baby was born, she then had two children under the age of two who were solely dependent upon her. This was what she'd wanted, so why was she so overwhelmed by her responsibilities?

When she took a closer look, she realized that her own mother had been quite disconnected from her. Her mother had had five children and was overwhelmed herself. Janet was the youngest of the five. Her mother also relied upon the parenting information of the day, which said that children needed to be held only at certain times. As a baby, Janet was often left to cry when it wasn't time for her to be fed or changed. Janet's mother was also physically and emotionally abusive. As a result, Janet sometimes wanted to cling to her mother, but sometimes felt it was safer to stay away from her. Over the years, Janet's family had told her repeatedly that everyone thought she was a really good baby. They didn't realize that she was shut down and withdrawn most of the time.

When Janet began to encounter difficulties with her children's behaviors, she became overwhelmed. She would shut down or, conversely, become very angry and somewhat abusive. She was physically present with her kids, yet she was emotionally absent. She didn't know what to do or how to become the parent she wanted to be. She knew that she didn't want to do what her mother had done, but she didn't know what to do to stop the fighting between her children, the yelling, and the destructive behaviors. She was frozen.

Many parents find themselves in this situation, realizing that they do not have the model for the family they are trying to create. Their own blueprints or templates for relationship, what they experienced in their early years, don't provide an example of the loving home they want. The more challenged the parent is, the more challenging the child will be. When a child is also really disorganized—and all children are to some degree or another—their behaviors will become extreme, which will further overwhelm the parent who is following road maps that don't tell him or her how to reconnect. Their situation can become a horrible cycle of disconnection from which no one can seem to escape.

But there is a way out. Making changes in our family starts with how we interpret our children's behaviors on a daily basis, which is the topic of our next principle and chapter.

Questions to Ponder

- When you were growing up,
    - could you talk to your parents if something was bothering you?
    - what did you do when you were having a challenge in your life?
    - were you able to express your feelings and share your emotions to get support?

- What kind of a relationship do you want with your child?

- Is it safe for your child to express feelings? Is your child's expression of feelings hurting anyone?

- What happens in your world when you're upset? Do you talk? Yell? Withdraw?

- Consider the patterns in your family growing up. Are there any similarities to the patterns you are experiencing now in your family with your own children? What about your partner's family?

Chapter Six

How We Interpret Our Children's Behavior

Principle 5: Parental interpretation of behaviors comes from both a conscious and subconscious place, resulting in positive or negative neurophysiologic feedback loops.

Most parenting information focuses only on the child's behavior and the "best" parental response to it. Rarely is there mention of the underlying dynamics that contribute to how parents feel about their response or about the child. But since we are not just staying on the surface with behaviors, we are going to dive in deep and take a closer look at the relationship between the parent and child.

When our child does something—literally anything—we parents connect it, both consciously and unconsciously, to things that happened in our past. Memory doesn't work in a linear fashion; in our brain, something that happened this morning may not take precedence over something that happened to us when we were five. In other words, our brain may time travel with or without our conscious awareness or permission.

For example, for months my boys were often fighting in the backseat of the car when we tried to go anywhere. Whatever items could be found were flying around the back of the car and sometimes into the front seat, accompanied by yelling and misery. I found myself going back and forth between ignoring my sons' behaviors because I didn't know what to do, yelling at the boys to stop it, and pulling over and waiting until the fighting stopped (but waiting in an angry, disappointed, moping sort of way—not with any sort of understanding or compassion). Nothing really worked, though, and I found myself feeling increasingly frustrated.

I began writing in my journal about this experience, asking myself what this situation reminded me of and why I was feeling so helpless. What I realized was that I had been in this situation as a child with my two brothers, who fought constantly in the backseat of my parents' station wagon. (You remember the kind of wagon with the wood paneling, right?) When my own children started fighting in the backseat, I was time traveling back to the situation with my brothers, in which my mother had felt helpless. I realized that the previous situation and the helplessness didn't belong to me at all. I realized that if I stayed present in my current vehicle and out of my parents' station wagon, I would have a much better chance of solving this problem.

The next time the kids started to fight, I worked to remind myself that I was in the present moment. I looked at my steering wheel; I was in the driver's seat, not a helpless child passenger in the backseat. I was the adult here, and that meant that I could do something to make this situation better. I took some nice deep breaths and decided that it was simply unsafe to drive with so much commotion in the back. Without the erratic swerving onto the shoulder that I had previously tried, I pulled the car off the road and continued to focus on my breathing. I knew if I spoke too soon, I would not respond in the way I wanted to. My knee-jerk reaction was to start yelling at them and flailing my hand around in the backseat, but I knew that wasn't the best way to handle this behavior.

When I was as calm as I was going to be, I said, "Wow! Sounds like you boys are pretty upset right now. I'd really like to hear what you both have to say about what's going on here." They both froze and looked at me as if an alien had taken over their mother and asked them if they wanted a pizza. As their shock lifted, I listened as they tried to talk over one another, kept breathing to calm myself, and took in their accounts of how the other one did him wrong. I validated how they were each feeling, saying, "That must be frustrating to have your brother touching your game," and, "You don't like your brother very much right now. That's understandable." I didn't try to fix the conflict for them. I just listened and validated each child's own unique perspective. When they were done, I invited them to suggest how this situation could be remedied, since Mommy cannot drive when there is yelling.

They thought for a moment, and my older son suggested that he move up to the front seat. They both agreed to this solution. My younger son suggested they listen to a book on CD that I always had in the car. I had forgotten that we even had those CDs!

We got back onto the road, my older son sitting next to me in the front, our *Pirate Stories* CD playing, and three people experiencing a positive outcome to what started as an unconscious replaying of my own childhood scenes.

Feedback Loops

I was able to resolve my backseat dilemma by changing the feedback loop that was at play. **Feedback loops** are patterns of communication, spoken and unspoken, including actions, body language, facial expressions, and how we feel about ourselves and our children at the time. It is important to recognize that intention, unconscious communication, and body language speak just as loudly as, if not louder than, our spoken words. When our spoken and unspoken communication don't match, our meta-communication, or the sum of our unspoken communication, is the loudest. "Actions speak louder than words" is a phrase most people are familiar with.

Here's an example: Try to hit your hands on a table with some force and wrinkle your face up in an angry way. Now repeat the movement with your hands, but say, "I love you." What is actually communicated? The words expressing love are meaningless after the power of the unspoken actions.

The word *neurophysiologic* (comprised of *neuro*, meaning the nervous system, and *physiologic,* indicating the body) is important here because we can recognize that we aren't just communicating with our words, but also with our thoughts, our feelings, and our patterns of energy perceived within our bodies and our nervous systems. The work of the Heartmath Institute in Boulder Creek, California, helps us to understand that even when we aren't speaking to each other, our bodies are constantly communicating to one another, especially through our hearts. According to Heartmath, when we're out of coherence with our body-mind (our subconscious and conscious), everyone around us, including our family members, feels our negative energy (whether we say something out loud or not), and as a result, we're likely to find ourselves in the downward, negative spiral with our kids. When we can shift ourselves back into a state of harmony within our bodies and our minds, we can exit the merry-go-round.

I was able to return myself to an internal state of harmony by focusing on my breathing and consciously reminding myself that I was an adult and in the driver's seat. My intention was to create peace and harmony on the car ride, along with safety for all of us. But my original actions, my feelings, and my words were not in alignment with my intentions because I was interpreting my current situation the same way I had interpreted my mother's situation when I was a child. When I realized what was happening, I was able to shift my interpretation of the situation. (This wasn't my brothers fighting when I felt I could do nothing. This was my own children in need of some guidance.) And then I was able to respond in a way that was congruent with my intentions.

Becoming aware of my own internal negative feedback loop and my subconscious interpretation of the situation ("I am powerless against fighting in the car"), and then changing my interpretation, feelings, and response to the situation, did take some time. Sometimes we require an objective, loving listener to help us sort out the situation. In this case, I put pen to paper and began by asking myself what this situation reminded me of and why I was feeling so helpless. Once I had some clarity, I was able to respond differently in the moment. And when I was able to actually connect with my children and thus create peace in my car, I felt empowered. Healing from the past is empowering.

I had been slipping into a very old negative feedback loop from a situation long ago. I tried all the "solutions" my mom had tried and experienced the same results she had. My boys and I were traveling around and around in this situation, and no one's needs were being met. I was doing things in a negative state to try to stop negative behavior, and as a result, I only added negativity. I needed to realize that I was the one who could change the negative cycle.

Everyday feedback loops—those situations we find ourselves stuck in and that don't go the way we want them to go—are opportunities for us to discover our own stuck points and to heal from our own past traumas and times when we were otherwise disempowered. Embrace your opportunities!

Judgments and Interpretations

My son bared his teeth and moved his head in toward mine so that our foreheads nearly touched. For a split second, I thought he was going to bang into my head. With that realization dawning, I decided he was being playful and just moving in to kiss me. I reached toward him and kissed him. He then smiled and told me how much he loved me. A few minutes later, after he had gone back off to the other room to play, it occurred to me how differently that situation would have gone if I had decided that his action was a threat to me. How many times do our interpretations of our child's behavior lead us down the path to more disconnection?

We interpret our child's behaviors hundreds of times per day, mostly unconsciously. If things are generally going well with our child and with us, we're more likely to have the patience and the wherewithal to interpret our child's behaviors in a positive light. If we're feeling overwhelmed or if our relationship with our child is generally not going so well, we're more likely to interpret our child's behaviors in a negative light, regardless of the child's intention. I'm not saying that our children are always completely innocent or that they don't need to learn to communicate with us effectively to get their needs met. I'm pointing out that sometimes just a simple shift in our interpretation of what our child is saying or doing can make things go in a positive direction.

We are constantly making observations, judging behaviors, and then interpreting what our children do—all in the blink of an eye. Many of these judgments and interpretations are based upon previous circumstances and how things worked out for us (or our loved ones) in the past. The primitive part of the brain is responsible for screening all the things happening around us for possible threats. If I had allowed my amygdala (the primitive part of my brain responsible for the fight, flight, or freeze response) to take over in the situation with my son above, I would have fought back, run away, or frozen. Because I was aware of myself and realized that my five-year-old wasn't really a threat, I was able to interpret his behavior in a different way that had a positive outcome.

"My daughter is manipulating me!" "He did that to me on purpose just to make me mad!" "I'm the parent, and he needs to listen to what I say!" Phrases like these are common among today's parents. They are remnants of another age in which we did not fully understand brain development and what is really going on in the minds of our young children. We often overlay adult thinking onto what we are seeing from our children, even when they are not capable of this kind of complex thought. These kinds of phrases only create more disconnection in relationships because they reflect a judgment: we judge that our child is wrong or bad. But what if we asked ourselves what is the best possible interpretation for what our child just did? When we start to shift our interpretations and change our language to give our children the benefit of the doubt, there is the possibility of change.

Our children are always doing the best they can do at any given time. Parents don't always agree when I make this statement. But let me ask you this: Are you always doing the best you can in any given situation? (Not that you always handle things perfectly, but do you have good intentions?) Do you set out to do a lousy job and make everyone around you upset? I'd be surprised if you said yes. Our children want to please us, even if it doesn't look like it sometimes. They need us to hold the higher consciousness for them, to know and feel that they are doing their best. They need our support and our guidance, not harsh words and criticism.

Shifting Our Interpretations: Listening to Our Thoughts, Changing Our Words

As we begin to shift our interpretation of our child's actions, we may feel challenged. We may have words and thoughts that come into our minds when our child says or does something, and maybe these words actually come out of our mouths: "You can't do that to me!" "I'm the parent, and you have to listen to what I say without question!"

Where do these thoughts and words come from? Are they really valid? Does it really matter if our child doesn't have her napkin in her lap right this second? If you've told her in the past to use the napkin, do you interpret her action as a willful disobedience, or do you see her as a child who may need some reminders to help putting her napkin in her lap become a habit?

Paying Attention to Our Inner Voice

Paying attention to our own inner dialogue and pausing before opening our mouths doesn't mean that we don't teach our children what is appropriate, but rather that we are aware of where we are coming from and that we teach our children through gentle reminders and through modeling what we want our children to do. When we are caught up in our own past experiences and playing the old tapes of our own childhood, we are out of the present moment. So hit the pause button and listen to your internal dialogue before you speak.

Pausing to listen to yourself and making sure you're present in the moment isn't something that you're going to do perfectly right away, and that's OK. It took a long time for these patterns to become a part of you, so it will naturally take time to create your new patterns. It takes thirty days to create a new neural pathway in your brain and for a neural pathway that isn't used to begin to recede. Listening to your thoughts before speaking becomes easier and easier as the new neural patterns become established. Remember that everything starts with awareness. What situations do you struggle with the most? What does your child do that drives you crazy? Pay attention. You're on the treasure hunt, looking for the golden clues.

Watching Our Words

Positive, affirming statements about our children go a long way toward creating a connected relationship. When we use words that affirm our child's innate goodness and willingness to help, we will begin to see more of those traits in our child. When we focus on the negative things we don't like, our child will begin to feel that he actually is "lazy," that he "never listens," that he "is a dreamer," that he "has ADHD and can't pay attention." When you begin to be more mindful of the words you use to describe your child and the words you use to talk to your child, you can start making shifts in your relationship.

We can create a new interpretation of nearly any situation if we can get outside of our own past interpretations. A toddler picking up a shoe that doesn't belong to him becomes an opportunity to thank him for helping to bring you the shoe. An older child who doesn't have her napkin in her lap becomes a child who simply forgot to put her napkin in her lap today. A yelling child can become a child who is overwhelmed by his day and needs support and nurturing to move back to a state of regulation and calm.

As we learn to pause and to look at our interpretation of our child's behavior, we begin to see opportunities to create more connection just by shifting how we look at the situation.

Feedback Loops: Getting Off the Merry-Go-Round

Have you had those situations in your life where something
negative happens, you react to it in a way you would rather not,
your child gets more upset, which makes you more upset, and
you go round and round like this? And you know it is going to
happen every time your child does _____ (fill in the blank).
Maybe it is your tween rolling his eyes at you or your toddler
throwing all her food on the floor (again). For me, it was my
boys fighting in the backseat of the car. We all have our triggers—
those situations that send us over the edge. How do we stop them
from sending us into this negative cycle?

First, we need to become aware of ourselves and aware
of our own emotional state. Are we calm and connected (in
green-light brain state)? Are we teetering on a yellow light, not
heeding our own caution signs and our need to slow down and
connect? Or are we in a blazing red-light state, sailing on through
the intersection even though there are clear signs saying that
stopping would be in order?

To help you become more aware of yourself and your
states, ask yourself, "What do I look like when I am calm and
connected? What does it look like or feel like when I shift into
a yellow-light state?"

One mom I spoke to claimed to have only green and red
lights. As we talked more about a specific incident in which she
had been very reactive and yelled at her children (which she
normally didn't do), we started to identify the signs that came
before her self-proclaimed "adult tantrum." For her, the signs
were physical. She noticed that she felt feverish and that her
heart was pounding before she fell apart. I pointed out that her
body was telling her that she was angry before she even opened
her mouth. I suggested that she share this information with her
husband and her older daughter, asking for their help in identifying these, her yellow lights. As it turned out, her oldest daughter,
who was twelve, was very aware of her mom's emotional state
and could identify easily when things were starting to not go so

well. Mom and Bella decided that something Bella could do if she noticed Mom was starting to struggle was to make her some tea. The next week when we talked, Mom reported that her daughter prepared her a lot of chamomile tea! This mom at first needed a little help identifying when she was struggling, and her daughter was willing to help her in this regard.

As we become more aware of what is happening and what specific situations challenge us the most, we may take the time to write about our experiences. Writing about both our thoughts and feelings is important to our healing process, says James Pennebaker in his book *Opening Up*. Writing helps us become aware of our unconscious interpretations of our children's behaviors. The most important part is not to censor your writing in any way; remember, the paper will never judge what you have to say. Plus, a pen and paper are usually readily available in the present moment. Another great way to sort through your experiences is to find a friend, partner, or other safe person, such as a really good therapist, who can listen to you talk about the situation without judging you or fixing it for you.

As you begin to write or share, you may find yourself shifting from the present situation to other times you have felt the same way. That other time may be a relatively recent situation, or it may be from the distant past. Let it come out and find its voice. It will tell you what you need to know. As you continue this process, you may clarify your beliefs about your current situation, as well. Does your child remind you of your little sister who never respected your things? Do you see glimpses of yourself in your own child and want to stop his or her behavior before it spirals out of control? What are your fears? What will happen if the behavior doesn't stop?

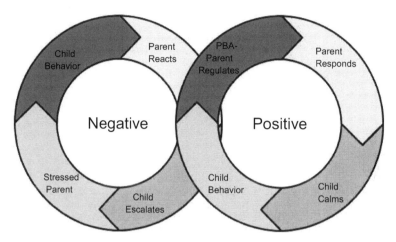

Figure 2: Exploring the feedback loop merry-go-round; changing a negative feedback loop to a positive.

Shifting Your Interpretation of Your Children's Behaviors

- Take note of your own emotional state. *"I'm on a red light!"* Say it out loud.

- Foster your awareness of what situations trigger you to shift out of connection and calm (green light) and into feeling overwhelmed (red light). *"I'm upset that Kyle threw his food all over the floor again!"*

(continued)

- Write or share with a safe person your thoughts and feelings regarding the situations that pull you out of your green-light state. "Every time Kyle throws his food down, I get really upset. I feel tension in the center of my body and in my shoulders. How dare he do this to me!"

- Discover your interpretation of your child's behavior and what you are afraid will happen if it doesn't stop. "My interpretation is that he is doing this to me on purpose. He thinks it is funny that he makes more work for me. It isn't fair! If I don't stop this behavior right now, it will never stop!"

- Release your old interpretation and the feelings that go with it. (See chapter seven on releasing feelings for more explanation.) "I realize that I am angry with my baby because I feel he is doing something I don't enjoy. I feel powerless in this situation, and I feel the need to control his behaviors. It doesn't work for me because I keep finding myself in an angry place. And it doesn't work for Kyle because he also deserves to be treated with respect."

- Create a new interpretation for your child's behavior. "Kyle is only fourteen months old. His job is to explore the world and to discover what happens when he does things. Throwing the food on the floor is part of being a one-year-old and not something personal he is doing to me to upset me."

(continued)

> • Visualize the situation having a different outcome, noticing what you can change to make it turn out differently. "Babies need to explore their world, and they also need to eat. I can offer him smaller portions of food to eat at a time, so that if he does drop some, it won't make a huge mess. If he is consistently throwing food on the floor, I'll know that he is probably communicating that he is done eating. That will be my cue to start cleaning up from the meal."

Questions to Ponder

- What situations really trigger you out of a green-light state, or calm, connected place?

- What does it look like for you when you are shifting into a yellow-light state?

- What does it look like for you when you are shifting into a red-light state?

- What calms you down in the moment?

- What strategies can you use to understand your own interpretation of your child's behavior? Are you a writer? Do you have safe friends, a spouse, or relatives with whom you can share your thoughts and feelings?

- What are you afraid will happen if you don't stop your child's behavior right now?

Chapter Seven

Feelings: Messages from Our Internal Guidance System

Principle 6: All individuals have a right and a responsibility to learn to express their feelings appropriately. Feelings allow us to connect to our internal guidance system.

Few parents find navigating the landscape of feelings to be easy. Perhaps one of the most misunderstood aspects of parenting, the language of feelings and what its role is in helping our children to find their way is something we all need guidance to understand. While growing up, most of us received messages telling us that our feelings were inappropriate or something that must be fixed. Yet the expression of feelings is normal, and feelings are the key to truly connecting to one another in a deep and meaningful way.

Feelings have an important place in our lives. They let us know when something isn't right or that all is well. Feelings let us become aware of situations where action may be needed.

Feelings are the felt sense of an emotion in the body. Many people express a feeling in words, but are disconnected from the physical sensations that correlate to certain emotions. Someone may say, "I'm so sad about this," yet not be connected to the hurt their stomach is holding. Emotion is energy in motion, and this motion is the bubbling up or physical way we experience feelings. This energy needs a place to go so that it doesn't become stuck in our physical bodies. When emotions are stopped, we can become stuck physically, emotionally, mentally, and socially.

As adults, some of us have learned that it isn't acceptable to express feelings, and we tend to hold them in until we just can't hold them in any longer. When your child is feeling mad, perhaps you can clearly see that your child's whole body is expressing the mad feelings inside. Young children usually do not yet possess the capacity to suppress their emotions, so they don't filter the expression of their emotions.

The emerging field of psychoneuroimmunology looks at the sensations in the body as the way the body communicates the feelings it holds. Louise Hay is famous for her *You Can Heal Your Life* book series, in which she identifies body sensations and signals as specific messages from the body-mind. Feelings and emotions held in the body long enough can and often do become disease unless they find a healthy expression. The physical discomforts in your body are not coincidences; they are messages. Our society is full of diseases that are really stress related and have dysregulation at their root. Ninety-five percent or more of psychiatric disorders have at their root a chronic inability to regulate the nervous system and, consequently, feelings and behavior.

If feelings are so important, why do we have such a difficult time with our feelings? The answer to this question begins with our own childhood experiences.

Learning to Handle Our Feelings

How did others handle your feelings when you were growing up? How did the adults around you react when you expressed your feelings? What happened when your parents or siblings were angry, upset, sad, happy? What happened to you? Were feelings allowed? Were they encouraged?

Recently I was teaching a class and asked these questions. Most of the participants said that, in one way or another, they had learned that all or some of their feelings were inappropriate. One mom reported that it was all right for her father to have angry outbursts, but no one else was allowed to express any feelings. Another woman shared that her mom was comfortable with her feelings of sadness, but her mom immediately shut her down if she expressed any anger. Some people grow up watching others express their feelings as a way of taking control of situations or express feelings in ways that were abusive.

Very few people have had a parent say to them, "It is all right to cry. I'll sit with you and hold you until you're feeling better." Or, "Tell me how angry you are about that!" When we haven't had those positive experiences with our feelings, it is difficult for us to give them to our children, even if we want to, and we don't know how to encourage the healthy expression of feelings in our children.

Many times, this disconnection from our inner experience started with our parents' reaction or lack of response to us expressing our feelings in infancy. Some parents are completely disconnected from their children's cries. If, as adults, we are desensitized to the upsets of those we love, our caregivers were probably disconnected from us when we were infants and young children, either because they didn't know how to deal with our upsets or they were following the advice of the day, which said responding to a baby's needs was spoiling the baby.

Connecting With Our Feelings: A First Step

We don't want to repeat our negative childhood experiences with our children, so we need to first connect with our own pain from those experiences. To begin connecting with your childhood feelings, think about a time when a teacher or other adult smiled at you or went out of their way to do something nice for you. Now think of a time when a classmate or sibling called you a name or said they didn't want to play with you because of how you looked or acted. Just touch lightly on this latter feeling—just enough that you remember how it felt—and let it go.

Connecting with and acknowledging our feelings from our childhood makes us more aware of ourselves and our own patterns so that we can stop the cycle and create something more positive in our own family.

Regulating Our Feelings and Behavior

We must be able to regulate ourselves at a body level in order to regulate our feelings and our behavior. If we are living in a state of dysregulation, we may find that our feelings are blocked (in which case we're hypoaroused) or our feelings fly out quickly and without warning (we're hyperaroused). It is only through regulation that we can express feelings in a way that doesn't hurt anyone, including ourselves. We own our own feelings. They may have been *triggered* by a situation with another person, but they weren't *caused* by another person or event. When we are expressing our feelings in a healthy way, we remain empowered. We use feelings to recognize unmet needs in our life, rather than as signals that someone has done something to us and we are the victim.

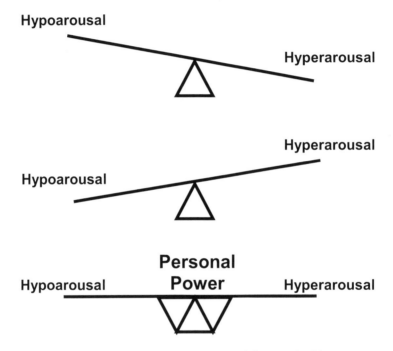

Figure 3: When we are in balance with our feelings, we're able to respect our own needs and feelings and respect the needs and feelings of others. When one person in a family is hyperaroused, someone else is likely to be hypoaroused to balance the energy. The reverse is also true. When one person is hypoaroused, another family member is likely to be hyperaroused.

Feelings as Our Guide: Shifting into New Behaviors Through Awareness

- Become aware of your thoughts and feelings by checking in with your physical body.

- Express your thoughts and feelings to a safe person. (A safe person is one who will allow you to completely express your feelings and thoughts without needing to stop you by invalidating, shaming, distracting, or trying to fix the hurt.) Alternatively, write down your thoughts and feelings without censoring.

- Visualize new actions, practice new thoughts, and allow feelings to shift.

- Practice pausing (i.e., pause before acting).

- Practice new behaviors, first in your head, then in real life. Examples of new behaviors include creating a space for sharing, connecting daily with your child when things aren't overwhelming, or responding differently to a challenging situation you're experiencing with your child.

- Be kind and gentle with yourself when you return to previous patterns. Remember that you have another opportunity to reconnect with your child, and reconnecting after a disconnection is part of what makes an attachment strong.

What Does a Healthy Expression of Feelings Look Like?

The most difficult part of learning to express our feelings appropriately is recognizing when someone else is doing so. We have seen healthy, appropriate expressions of feelings so seldom in our lives that we don't know for sure when it's happening, much less how to model it for our own children.

Emotions need an avenue of expression, or they and their energy become trapped in our physical bodies. Expressing emotions doesn't mean encouraging our child to hurt other people when they're mad, but helping them learn how to move through the emotional energy and refrain from labeling those emotions as good or bad. Emotions are energy, and that energy needs an outlet, much like lightning needs a place to ground into the earth. Lightning isn't inherently good or bad, but lightning can move through objects in a way that hurts sometimes. This is why we have lightning rods to direct the energy into the earth, where it won't hurt anyone or anything. In the same way, we need to help our children learn how to allow the energy of their emotions to move through them in a way that doesn't hurt anyone, including themselves. And to help and support them as they learn, we need to learn how to do this for ourselves.

In general, the expression of the feelings needs to be respectful of ourselves and respectful of others' feelings and needs. Let's walk through an example using the familiar fairy tale of the Three Bears.

Once upon a time, there were three bears: Papa Bear, a stereotypical large, loud bear, who is usually hyperaroused; Mama Bear, the stereotypical small, quiet bear, who is usually hypoaroused; and Baby Bear, the only regulated person in the family. (Baby Bear is actually not a baby at all, but an emotionally mature teen bear. Let's say Baby Bear is able to express his feelings in a way that was respectful to others, probably because he spent much of his time with his regulated grandmother, who lived next door.)

One day, Mama Bear, who knew Papa Bear got cranky when he didn't eat his breakfast early enough in the morning, made some hot porridge so he wouldn't get mad. She made a big bowl for Papa Bear, a medium-sized bowl for herself, and a small bowl for Baby Bear.

The porridge was too hot. Papa Bear exploded in anger at having to wait for his breakfast to cool and went into a rant about how hungry he was and that no one seemed to respect his needs.

Mama Bear grew very quiet and still, feeling very afraid.

Baby Bear looked at his papa and said, "You must be very hungry to act like that. I'm sorry that you're so hungry and that breakfast isn't ready yet. Would you like an apple while you're waiting?"

Papa Bear grabbed an apple and took an angry bite, baring his teeth as he chewed. Mama Bear suggested very quietly that maybe a walk would do them all some good, so they went outside to go for a walk while the porridge cooled.

While they were out, along came Goldilocks. She made her rounds, eating the porridge, sitting in the chairs, and sleeping in the beds. When the bears returned, they walked into the kitchen and looked at the bowls of porridge.

Papa Bear exploded, "Who's been eating my porridge? Was it you?" He looked at both Mama and Baby Bear.

Mama Bear grew quiet again, unable to speak.

Baby Bear spoke up and said, "I find it difficult to feel safe when you are yelling. I can see that you're upset about your porridge. I know you're very hungry, and it was a surprise to see that your porridge was touched while we were on our walk. I'm wondering if you could say that differently?"

Papa Bear took a deep breath and tried again, "What happened to my porridge?"

Baby Bear looked at his mama and said, "Mama, you look upset that someone has also eaten your porridge. How are you feeling right now?"

Mama Bear looked at Baby Bear, took a deep breath, and said, "I'm hungry, too. Who could have eaten my porridge?"

Baby Bear looked at his bowl and realized that someone had eaten all of his porridge. "I'm really upset that someone ate all my porridge! My goodness! Whoever it was must have been very hungry."

The family moved into the next room to sit down together and figure out what to do next. As they entered the room, Papa Bear yelled, "Who's been sitting in my chair?"

Mama Bear hid her face in her shirt and started rocking from side to side. Papa Bear held the sides of his face with his hands and moaned.

Baby Bear said, "That was a surprise to see that someone has been sitting in your chair, wasn't it? What's that about for you?"

Papa Bear said, "It's my chair. Who would sit in it? Why would they sit in it?" Papa Bear began to whimper. Underneath his loud voice, he was really feeling scared that someone could have been here in his house.

Baby Bear turned to Mama Bear. "Mama, it's really scary to see that someone has been sitting in your chair, isn't it? Tell me how that feels to you."

Mama Bear took a deep breath and said, "Who could be doing this? Don't they know that it isn't OK to go into someone else's house?"

Just then, Baby Bear looked at his chair. "My favorite chair has been broken," he said, as tears of sadness ran down his cheeks. "This is the chair that Grandpapa made for me when I was small. Who could have done this?" He allowed himself a few minutes to cry and feel sad about what had happened to his favorite chair. When he was feeling better, he picked up the pieces of his chair and gently put them on the table.

Next, the bears went upstairs and looked at their beds. This time Papa Bear paused and took a nice deep breath. "Someone has been sleeping on my bed! That makes me angry that someone would do that. Who would do that?" Taking another deep breath, he calmed himself back down.

Mama Bear looked at her bed and said, "Oh my, I'm so scared. Someone has been sleeping in my bed, too."

Baby Bear cried out, "Someone has been sleeping in my bed, too, and there she is now!" Baby Bear walked over to Goldilocks and took a deep breath, pausing before he said anything. When he spoke, his words surprised everyone. "You look really frightened. We aren't going to hurt you. Why are you in our house?"

Goldilocks, who had expected anger and, at first glance, feared that the bears would eat her, stopped and looked at Baby Bear. After all, she had come into their house uninvited. "You're not mad?" she asked.

Baby Bear replied, "Clearly, you're here for a reason. It isn't OK to come into someone else's home uninvited, though. Next time, please knock. If you were hungry and tired, we would have happily shared our porridge and given you a place to rest." Then, to Papa and Mama Bear, he said, "Let's all go downstairs and get something to eat, and she can tell us all about how she happened upon our house."

And so they did.

In our story, Baby Bear was able to model and redirect his parent's hyperaroused and hypoaroused reactions to the new situations that were happening. The loud, angry outbursts of Papa Bear became quieter expressions of his needs and feelings. Mama Bear's shut-down response shifted into a verbal communication of her needs and feelings, rather than just trying to please her husband to avoid his angry outbursts.

When we first start our journey of becoming more aware of our own feelings, it may be that all we can do for a while is handle our own feelings. If we have been holding back our emotions for a while, we may need the support of someone trained to help guide this process of opening up to our feelings (the felt sense in the body) and emotions (the energy behind the feelings). With time, practice, and patience with ourselves, we will learn to become more aware of our own emotional state, recognize our needs, and decide upon an action to move ourselves forward. Eventually, we will be able to also allow others to have their own feelings about the situations in their lives as well, and we will be able to support our own children through the process. If our feelings tend to explode, we may need additional support to connect with the more tender feelings beneath the outbursts (fear, sadness, vulnerability) and how we are protecting ourselves with outward expressions of anger.

Supporting Our Children as They Express Feelings

If we, as parents, can understand that feelings are messages from our inner guidance systems and learn to express our own feelings in healthy ways, we can not only benefit ourselves, but also model these behaviors for our children. When we can learn that our own feelings are all right and how to move through our feelings in a positive way, we can teach our children to learn to interpret the signals their bodies are sending and accept their friendly guidance. Parenting brings up strong feelings for most parents, giving us many opportunities every day to experience feelings based on the things our children say and do. How we handle those feelings and how we express those feelings shows our children what to do with their own feelings, positive and negative.

I was recently on a plane and listening to a mother and her twelve-year-old son talking. The boy and his mother were on a trip for the birth of the boy's cousin, and the mother's sister was in labor. He had been told only that they were going for the birth, apparently, but no other details had been discussed. The conversation went something like this:

> **Mom.** When we get there, I'm going to the hospital to be with my sister while she has her baby. You're going to need to go spend time with your grandmother because you can't stay at the hospital.

> **Boy,** *sounding surprised.* Why not? Why can't I be there when she has her baby?

> **Mom,** *clearly uncomfortable with the idea herself.* Well, that's kind of a personal thing.

> **Boy.** Are you going to be in there?

> **Mom.** Yes. And you can't stay in the waiting room of the hospital by yourself, so you'll need to go with Grandma.

> **Boy.** I don't want to go with Grandma.

> **Mom.** Why?

> **Boy.** I don't like her.

> **Mom.** Don't say that! That's not nice.

> **Boy.** But I want to stay with you, and I want to see the baby being born.

> **Mom.** You're going with Grandma and that's the end of it.

Sounds like a fairly common interchange, doesn't it? This boy isn't going to go in and see the baby being born without his aunt's permission, so we're going to assume that a limit really does need to be set here. But what about setting a limit while still respecting the boy's feelings? What would that look like? Maybe like this:

> **Mom.** When we get there, I'm going to the hospital to be with my sister while she has her baby. You're going to need to go spend time with your grandmother because you can't stay at the hospital.

> **Boy.** Why not? Why can't I be there when she has her baby?

> **Mom,** *pausing, noticing that her son apparently expected to be able to be there for the birth, then checking in with her own feelings before she speaks.* I'm sorry. I didn't realize that you thought that you were going to be able to see the birth.

> **Boy.** Yeah, I've never seen a baby born before.

> **Mom.** I know you haven't. Birth is a really personal sort of process, and your aunt just isn't comfortable with anyone being in there besides me and the doctors. It is important for my sister to be as comfortable as possible, or the labor could stop and the baby won't come out! At the same time, it is important that you know that your feelings matter to me, too. Would it be all right if we called you as soon as the baby is born to come and meet your new cousin?

Boy. Well, where am I going to be if I'm not with you?

Mom. Grandma is going to come and get you.

Boy. I don't want to go with Grandma.

Mom. Why not?

Boy. I don't like her.

Mom, *pausing to acknowledge the feelings she is observing before speaking.* Sounds like you don't want to go with Grandma.

Boy. No, I really want to stay with you. Grandma is boring.

Mom. I see. Sounds like this just isn't what you had expected when we got on the plane.

Boy. No, it isn't what I expected.

Mom, *pausing to really connect with his feelings.* I know you're disappointed.

Boy. What am I going to do with Grandma?

Mom. She's going to take you out to lunch anywhere you want to go. Then you two can decide what you want to do until the baby comes. I'll call you as soon as the baby is born, and you can come meet your new cousin.

Boy. I guess that's all right. You'll really call as soon as the baby is born?

Mom. Yes, of course. It is so wonderful to see a brand new baby. You know, thinking about birth reminds me of when you were born.

Boy. Tell me the story again.

In this scenario, the way Mom handled her son's feelings allowed him to process new information without judgment. She models for her son how to respectfully handle someone else's upsets, and the words she chose and the way she expressed herself allowed them to connect rather than disconnect. Mom also maintained the limit she'd set: that it wasn't all right for him to attend the birth and that he was going to go with his grandmother. When our children are given support as they process how they feel about a situation, they will naturally come to the other side of the feelings, and then you can support them in processing new information, if necessary.

Note: When children haven't previously been supported as they express their feelings, it may take some time for them to move through the expression of the feelings in a connected space with you and into the calm afterwards. More time might be needed because there may be a backlog of unexpressed feelings waiting for the opportunity to be heard and acknowledged. With time and practice, parents will become more adept at supporting their children, and the children will be able to express their feelings more quickly and easily.

Another note: Many well-meaning parents, myself included at one time, don't want their children to have to cry. We all want what is best for our children, but upsets are part of our existence. With very young children who can't tell us what is wrong, it is best to try to figure out what is happening with them.

But we can't always know, and we can't always fix what's bothering them, as in the case of a colicky baby. Sometimes *not* trying to fix what's wrong is the best way to truly connect with our children. Instead of always trying to fix their problems, we can take the opportunity to simply be present with our children and support them as they express the feelings they need to express, regardless of their age.

Button-Pushing Feelings and Boundaries

But what about those feelings that make us wish feelings weren't such an integral part of our humanity? What about the feelings that well up within us as we're parenting our children that feel intentional and manipulative?

Here's an example from my life. In the past, anger was an overwhelming feeling for me. It was challenging for me to feel anger, and I found it incredibly challenging when my son was feeling and expressing anger, particularly when he was angry with me. Since my son's expression of anger was very uncomfortable for me, I found myself unconsciously avoiding situations that would upset him. And I realized that I was walking on eggshells in my own home and not setting boundaries that he probably needed just to avoid the outbursts.

It took me a long while to really understand that allowing his feelings didn't mean that he got to do whatever he wanted because he was feeling a certain way. In fact, it usually meant that he was often too overwhelmed for whatever he wanted, and he needed me to reign him in a bit by setting a limit and allow him to "spill his hurts cup," as Pam Leo, author of *Connection Parenting* would say. He needed to express those feelings, and he needed me to hear him. He needed me to acknowledge his hurts and allow the fear and sadness that was masked beneath the anger to come to the surface. He didn't actually need the toy or the dinner out that he was demanding,

The Power of the Pause

When I began to change the way I was responding to my children, I started pausing because I didn't know what else to do. What I was doing wasn't working, but I didn't have a clearly defined new plan either. And I still had work to do on my own past so that I could see the present more clearly.

I believe I thought every situation warranted an immediate response, but there are very few actual parenting emergencies that require lightning reflexes and no thought. A child running into the road is an emergency. Even though it felt like an emergency, my older son speaking unkindly to his brother was not. The situation still needed attention, but there was time to pause before acting.

So I started pausing, and an interesting thing happened. Sometimes what I was so afraid was going to happen, didn't.

Sometimes it did, but it wasn't exactly like I thought it would be. I found I had time to think. I could sometimes even think of something helpful to do, which in turn created connection.

Sometimes I used the pause to reconnect to myself, my feelings, my thoughts, and my interpretations. Sometimes I just breathed. My family started changing right there in the pause.

Sometimes I got in only a small pause and then still did whatever reactionary thing I was going to do. But I celebrated the pause anyway. Big changes don't happen overnight, but rather through small, everyday victories—victories like the pause.

but he needed to be seen and heard and have someone feel what he was feeling with him.

For example, when my son was angry because he wasn't able to eat something due to his allergies, he didn't need someone to give him a piece of cake filled with off-limits ingredients. He needed someone to be with him and understand how hard that was for him. And he needed someone to feel it with him. I connected with his feelings—and him—quite by accident when I went on the same diet with him and eyed a brownie made with all the ingredients we could not eat with an intense longing right along with him. I felt the same thing he did. Because he had an ally, an amazing thing happened. He felt his feelings when they came up, but they didn't last long. He soon stopped asking if he could eat things that were clearly off limits, and he trusted that I would look out for him. Our relationship actually grew stronger not only because I set limits to keep him safe, but also because I was able to share his feelings with him.

Allowing our children to feel and express their feelings doesn't mean that we stop being the parent. We are the ones who are looking at all the options with their best interest at heart and making decisions for them until such a time that they can make decisions for themselves. My oldest son couldn't have many allergenic foods for a long time because they made him sick. I would have been irresponsible to let him have them anyway because he was upset by my limit. It was a hard lesson for this attachment parent, but one that I'm grateful to have had. I see many parents who are unable or unwilling to set limits when their children have strong feelings because these parents believe letting their children have their way is the best way to respect their children.

Looking out for our children doesn't mean setting limits for the sake of setting limits. But if you have strong feelings about something yourself, you're doing a disservice by not setting a limit and then getting upset with your child later. As Carrie

Contey remarked in an interview I did with her on boundaries with children, "It is far better for the child to have the tantrum than the parent to have the tantrum." Decide what is really important to you and set limits around those things when appropriate. Later, you'll be glad you did!

Marnie, mother of two tandem-nursing boys under three, was feeling particularly touched out. Her older son, Jake, was nursing more often than he did as a newborn, and Marnie was starting to feel more than a little crazy. On more than one occasion, she had snapped at Jake in frustration, and she was really starting to resent him and his needs. Recently, she found herself yelling at Jake when he asked to nurse yet again. Marnie needed to set a limit with Jake for the sake of their relationship. When I asked her to reflect on how often she would be happy to nurse Jake, she replied that she would be fine nursing first thing in the morning (her favorite time to cuddle with him), before and after his nap, and right before bed. But in between those times, Jake was likely to be unhappy.

Marnie decided to tell Jake stories about when he was a baby and needed to nurse often. She shared with him how happy she was to nurse him and hold him close. Then she explained that now, sometimes she wasn't happy nursing him (which he was already sensing, but which Marnie hadn't said), and she wanted to nurse him only when she was happy to do so. Though she was unwilling to nurse, she recognized that he needed her, and she was very willing to hold him and snuggle with him, or maybe tell him a story. She then shared with him the times she was happy to nurse and then told him that she is always there for him to snuggle with. He might not always be happy, and she's OK with his feelings.

The next time Jake asked to nurse in the middle of the day, Marnie gently reminded him that they weren't going to nurse until naptime. She was happy to hold him, rock him, and be sad with him. He cried, and she held him in her arms, crying with him. And when the wave of emotion passed for both of them, and they were feeling more settled, she read him one of his favorite stories. She felt so much more connected to him knowing that she hadn't gotten mad at him for having his needs and for simply making space for his feelings. When she did nurse him, she felt so much more connected to him. He weaned himself within a few months, feeling complete with his nursing relationship now that his mom was no longer pushing him away energetically when he was trying to connect through nursing. A more thorough discussion of limits and boundaries can be found in chapter eight: "Setting Limits While Honoring Feelings."

As I shared earlier, my feeling challenge as a parent was with my son's anger. For some parents, the challenge comes from their children crying and expressing disappointment, hurt, or sadness. What feelings are particularly challenging for you personally? What kinds of feelings and expressions from your child are most difficult for you? What about your partner?

Feelings and Our Inner Guidance System

We've all had really wonderful experiences feeling deeply connected to someone else. Perhaps we felt deeply connected to our significant other when we were married or dating, or we felt connected to our new baby when we gazed into her eyes for the first time. Those experiences are so rich in part because we have had other experiences that weren't so wonderful. We need a full range of emotions and experiences to really appreciate the joys in our lives.

Our feelings can help to guide us on our life journey and especially on our parenting journey. Our feelings can let us know when our life is out of balance, when we have unmet needs, or when something isn't right with our child and some sort of intervention is needed. Every day, I hear parents telling me how they feel about what is happening in their lives. They tell me when they're really concerned about their child's behavior or when they feel that behavior isn't really a problem and will work itself out. Some of you may call this intuition. I think of it as our inner guidance system, which is much like a GPS for parenting. Whatever you call it, our feelings are an essential part of how we all learn to find our way through our own unique parenting journey.

Sometimes when we've had a lot happen in our lives and not had the support we need to work our way through the overwhelming events we've experienced, we can feel mixed signals from our inner guidance system. The air around us is murky, and we feel unsure which path is right for us at the time. When you feel this way, remember that we all need one another to find our way, and sometimes an outside perspective can do wonders for helping us find our own way.

As we move through our own healing process, it becomes easier and easier to look inside ourselves and find what we need to do. When we can quiet the chatter and ground ourselves in this moment, the answer is often right there in front of us, waiting for the moment when we're quiet enough to listen.

Questions to Ponder

- How were feelings handled in your family when you were growing up? What were the "rules" regarding your expression of feelings? Was it different for happy feelings, angry feelings, and sad feelings? Was expressing feelings OK only if there was an obvious reason for the feeling? Were there different rules for your parents? For your siblings?

- How do you handle your child's feelings? Do you follow the old road maps showing how feelings were handled when you were growing up? Or have you created a new course for yourself and your children? What is your biggest challenge regarding your child's feelings?

Chapter Eight

Setting Limits While Honoring Feelings

Principle 7: Children need boundaries. We can set appropriate limits for our children while still respecting their needs and feelings—if we are aware of ourselves. (We can ask, for example, "Is this about me? Is this about them? Are my children communicating a need? Is the boundary I'm setting necessary, or is it an opportunity for me to grow?")

Perhaps the least understood guiding principle is about boundaries or limits. When we think of loving guidance and focusing on relationship, we sometimes think that means the children can do whatever they want. Or we think we need to let go of our own needs in order to meet our child's expressed needs and respect our child. Or perhaps we feel that the consequences of setting a limit with our child are going to be too great for us. So we co-sleep for longer than we really wanted to, let our children eat whatever they want to the point that their nutrition is suffering, or completely rearrange our lives so that we have the least amount of conflict with our child. Or maybe we set limits by disregarding how our child may be feeling.

I'm not saying that we ought not keep in mind what our child wants and needs. On the contrary, we need to keep our child's needs in mind when we make decisions that affect them. At the same time, we also need to respect our own needs so that we don't feel resentful of our child's needs usurping our own. The difference in relationship-focused limits is in how we present the limits and honor our child's feelings when a limit is set. Pam Leo, author of *Connection Parenting,* says that every *no* someone hears (notice I didn't say "your child hears") is a loss. That doesn't mean that we don't set limits, but it does mean that we respect the feelings our child is having when we need to use *no*.

Many loving parents are afraid to set boundaries with their children, either because of the flood of feelings that arise from the child when they do or because they are afraid to stifle their child. However, we can set limits while still being respectful. And there can be consequences without those consequences being a punishment. Limits are needed, but not at the expense of our children's basic needs, which include unconditional love and respect.

On the flip side, other parents react to their child's every action, or they try to control all of their child's behaviors. When parents do this, the child is less likely to explore the world. It is much better to create a safe environment for our children to explore than to constantly tell them no. As young children, we hear the word *no* many more times per day than we hear the word *yes,* and that means that our brains are really only hearing that we are unable to do things. Think of what believing that they *can't* do things or they aren't capable of them does as our children develop. We can strive toward finding a balance between respecting our needs and respecting our child's needs.

Parenting Beyond Behavior

Everywhere we look, from magazine articles to *Super Nanny* on television, we hear about the importance of structure and punishing our children when they are "naughty." I do agree that limits are needed, but not at the expense of our children's basic needs, which include unconditional love and respect. When we tell children that their behaviors are "bad," they internalize that *they themselves* are bad, even if it is not our intention. Why do we expect our children to "act better" after we make them feel worse?

This principle is different than you may think, so please read this section carefully.

When most parents are asked what discipline means, the most common answer is something that sounds like a punishment. "That child needs discipline!" generally means that a child is unruly and some type of pain (physical, emotional, or otherwise) should be inflicted upon the child so that the behavior will change. However, when we consult a dictionary, we see that the word *discipline* actually means, "to teach," and teaching doesn't imply making someone learn by imposing emotional isolation or pain. Children need discipline in the sense that they need someone to guide them, to let them know when something is appropriate or not, and to show them how to repair a relationship when an interaction didn't go as well as planned.

We can change behaviors by inflicting fear (of emotional or physical pain, abandonment, or separation) in our children, which creates disconnection, or by adding loving boundaries (by exhibiting understanding, keeping our children safe, or expressing curiosity about what is happening for our children), which creates connection. When we inflict pain on them, we are saying that stopping this behavior is more important than the children's need for connection. We are also saying that their behavior is something that just needs to go away and that it exists only to irritate us. We all parent from a place of fear when we're worried or stressed, especially because it is the paradigm in which most of us were raised. It is through connecting with ourselves, becoming compassionate with and for ourselves, that we can learn to parent from a place of love and connection. When we are coming from that place, our actions will naturally reflect our connection.

When Are Limits Necessary?

When do we need to set limits for our children?

Let's start with basic safety, because safety limits will help the need for other types of limit setting become more obvious. Children want to be safe. It is a basic need, as basic as the need for food and air and love. But children don't always know what is safe. It is our job to show them. I was at a parenting workshop, and the presenting therapist mentioned that our job as parents of children three years old and younger is to keep them alive until they are able to keep themselves safe. I would say that keeping our children safe doesn't end when our children are three. Our children don't have the wisdom that comes with age and the ability to make the best

(continued)

choices given all of the information. Children have a need for choice, but we need to make the initial choices for them so that the options they have to choose from are safe.

For example, my oldest son had a dairy allergy as a young child and wasn't able to eat anything with milk products. It would have been foolish for me to let him have free reign of all the food choices out there and expect that, as a four-year-old, he would know what was right for him. But I also respected his need for choice, especially when we would go places with other people eating things he couldn't have. I always included him in our grocery shopping and helped him to make healthy choices for himself, so that he could choose one of the foods that were good for his body when we were going to a birthday party or other situation where there would be foods he would be unable to eat.

I think most parents agree that it is unsafe for a child to play in a busy street. With very young children, it is probably too much to expect that they are going to make good choices for themselves when in that situation. So many parents put children into situations where they will not be tempted to run into the street, such as containing the child to a sling next to the parent's body or putting the child in a shopping cart or stroller. When parents do such things, they are being mindful of where their child is and what the child is capable of, while making decisions based upon the limit that needs to be set. They are meeting the needs of the child in a way that still puts the relationship first.

Setting Limits While Accepting Feelings

So how can we lovingly set limits with our children without using consequences and punishments? And how can we set these limits in a loving way that honors both our need to set them and our child's feelings about it?

Let's look at an example from my own life. When my youngest son, Josh, was five, he wanted to have a sugary treat when we were visiting his older brother's school. Because my son was having some issues with cavities, we had decided to limit his sugar, so I told him that he wouldn't be able to have the treat. Immediately, he started asking more loudly and trying to bargain with me about it. I returned to my no and told him that I knew it was difficult to want something that he couldn't have. I told him that I was sorry that he couldn't have it. And I meant it. He started crying softly in my arms, and I whispered in his ear, "I know it must be disappointing to see a treat that you really want and not be able to have it. I'd probably feel really sad." And I felt that it really was OK for him to be sad and, more importantly, I felt sad with him. After just a few minutes time, he was feeling better, and I offered him some other snacks that were fine for him to eat. He was able to shift his feelings and decided that he would keep the treat he couldn't eat for his brother to eat after school, which I thought was really nice of him. He ate his other snack, and that was the end of it.

Let's look at this scenario in smaller pieces:

1. My son wanted something that he couldn't have.

2. I knew I needed to set a limit for him.

3. I expressed the limit.

4. I listened to his feelings about the limit and validated his feelings. I felt the feelings with him. I didn't

change my mind (in this case), but I didn't try to stop his feelings, either.

5. I stayed present with him until he had moved through his wave of feelings, supporting him with my words and my intention.

6. I suggested alternatives only when he was ready to hear them. By staying quiet and in touch with my own inner guidance, I discerned when he was ready for them.

Here is another example of a situation when a limit needed to be adhered to and how one parent did so while respecting her children's feelings about it. Sarah had recently divorced and found herself suddenly responsible for the needs of her two children, Matt and Shelley, ages three and five, respectively. The court order required Matt and Shelley to visit their dad every Wednesday night, as well as every other weekend, and neither child wanted to go. In this situation, there was no choice in the matter for the children or their mom. At first, Sarah took the attitude that there was nothing anyone could do, so there was no point in complaining about it. She wanted her children to have a good relationship with their father and felt the children just needed to get over it. However, as the days stretched into months and the children's complaining seemed to be getting louder, she knew she needed to do something different. She sat them down for a conversation that went something like this:

> **Sarah.** Every week when we're getting ready for you to go to your dad's house, you two seem to have a hard time.

> **Matt.** Yeah, we don't want to go!

Sarah. I hear you saying that you don't want to go. Tell me what it is like when you don't want to go.

Matt. We miss you when we go to Dad's house. It's not the same when we're just with him.

Sarah. I hear you miss me. I miss you, too. It is hard when we're apart.

Shelley. We miss you. Why do we have to go?

Sarah. I know you miss me. You're wondering why you have to go. *She pulls them in close for hugs. Shelley starts to cry, followed by Matt.* I know it is hard. *She allows the space for their feelings to come out safely and to connect in this yellow-light state together.*

They all sit and cry together until the wave of feelings slows down on its own. There are very few words during this time.

Sarah, *sensing the connection between them and the yellow-light state changing back to green as everyone regulates.* Sometimes parents don't stay together, and that's a hard thing for everyone. Your dad still loves you and gets very little time with you right now. Tell me what you do when you're there.

As Sarah continued the conversation, she looked for any unmet needs so that she could further support her children through the separation and transitions. Were they feeling safe? Was the situation the best that it could be for everyone? As the time of the transition to their time with Dad neared, both children became more anxious. Sarah stopped, remembering that yellow lights need a nurturing response, and validated their feelings again.

> **Sarah.** I know it is so hard when it is time to go. Can I hold you until your dad gets here? *After a few minutes, she speaks again.* Let's figure out how we can stay close in our hearts while we're apart. Any ideas?

When the time came for Matt and Shelley to go, Sarah helped them to transition by having their dad engage playfully with them. The limit that the children must go with their dad was observed, and everyone's feelings and needs were respected.

It's Not About You

One reason we fail to respond to our children with connection, respect, and love is because we take our child's actions personally. This happens in the blink of an eye and is usually outside of our conscious awareness. For example, one night, my youngest (age five at the time) joined my husband and me in our bed at some point during the night. My husband's arms were wrapped around me and came over my body to where our son was sleeping. Suddenly, my son started kicking, and my husband raised his voice for him to stop. As I was right next to the sleeping child, I realized he was probably having a dream in which he was running. His kicking wasn't a personal attack against my husband.

Remember our first guiding principle? All behavior is a communication. In my lectures, I use the visual of an iceberg, part of which is visible above the water and part of which is under the water and unseen. I like to think of the top of the

Awareness of Ourselves

When we are calm, well rested, and fed, we are probably pretty good parents. We are able to handle the little bumps in the road—the lost shoes, the dawdling child—without much trouble. But when we're not on a green light ourselves, we may lose patience during the minor challenges of parenting. And when we are overwhelmed by our own life circumstances or by a situation our child throws our direction, our ability to parent in a connected way can be impaired. We need to learn to pay close attention to ourselves and our own needs and feelings so that we can model taking care of ourselves for our own children.

Sometimes the best thing we can do when we're having a hard time is to say this out loud: "I'm having a hard time today. What do I need right now?" And sometimes we need to let our children know (in age-appropriate terms) that we're having a hard day or a hard time. If you're grieving the loss of a parent, for example, let your child know that you're sad that Grandma died. When we're aware of our own feelings and can claim them as ours, we give our child a chance to understand that everyone has feelings, everyone has a bad day sometimes—even Mommy and Daddy. By asking what it is that we need, we're modeling awareness for those little watchful eyes, and by owning the feelings, we're showing them what healthy adults do with their feelings. This is true even if we're learning as we go, which we all are.

iceberg as our children's behaviors that we can see. Those might be the hitting, yelling, whining, throwing things, rolling their eyes, having an emotional meltdown, not going to sleep at bedtime, or any other behavior you can possibly think of. Those behaviors are what is on the surface, but what is underneath?

To show you what I mean, let's look at something that most of us have experienced as adults and that also often happens with our children. As an adult, I've had nights when I've had difficulty falling asleep. I knew the reason was that I had slept in late or I was worried about something and couldn't relax. Because of my own experience, I know that if my husband is having trouble falling asleep, he isn't keeping himself awake on purpose to bother me. So I might go into the bedroom and be with him for a little while and see if I could help him talk through whatever was on his mind and preventing him from falling to sleep.

Now imagine that the person who can't sleep is a child. How often do we (consciously or subconsciously) conclude that he or she is purposely not going to sleep—and probably staying awake just to annoy us? Or even if we think that something might be going on with our child, we're exhausted just thinking about our child being awake. Why can't she just go to sleep already?

My suggestion is that the child's behavior is communicating a need. Your child is communicating where he or she is in this moment. Are you listening? When you've remained awake after your bedtime, was it just because you were purposely trying to irritate someone by keeping yourself up? Would it have helped if someone reminded you that you had to get up early the next morning, so you'd better "hurry up and go to sleep"? Probably not.

Like us, our children sometimes have difficulty settling their bodies. And children are sometimes afraid of being alone. Children need to learn to calm down their own bodies, and they learn to do that with the help of a loving parent, not with isolation and threats. In my own experience, if my child hasn't had his needs for connection met during the day, he is much more likely to have difficulty settling at bedtime. I have found that if I go into the bedroom and spend time with my son as he goes to bed, he settles much more quickly than if I focus on consistently telling him to return to bed. Furthermore, I find that the whole thing is avoided the next day if I am more proactive about spending time with him before bedtime. If we don't take our child's behaviors personally, we're much more likely to be able to help her and meet her where she is in this moment—unable to sleep.

I can hear you saying, "OK, I understand that my child might be expressing a need with her behaviors, but it isn't all right for her to constantly get out of bed. If I'm not using a punishment or a consequence for her behavior, how will it ever stop?"

Good question! When our children are doing something that they know we don't like, we need to ask ourselves what their behavior is communicating before we can make a decision about how to respond. When we stop and breathe, calming ourselves, and perhaps even say to ourselves that our children's behavior is not personal—"This is not about me"—we can try to look at the world through our child's eyes.

Normally, we might react and yell at our child to get back in bed. But what if we responded like this dad with four-year-old Mandy?

> **Mandy,** *out of bed for the third time that night.* I need some water.

> **Dad,** *stopping to breathe and pause before acting, then saying, "This isn't about me" before starting to respond.* Honey, you normally do such a good job of listening when I ask you to do something, and this isn't like you. What's going

on with you that you keep getting out of bed?
Are you scared?

Mandy. Yes, I think there are monsters
under my bed that are going to eat me when
I fall asleep!

Dad. Oh my goodness! Monsters! I would have
a difficult time falling asleep if I thought there
were monsters under my bed, too! How scary!
What can I do to help you get off to sleep?

Mandy. Can you come into my room?

Dad. Sure, let's go see about those monsters.

This conscious parent was able to see that there was a message
behind the behavior and asked questions to join his daughter in
her world where monsters are real and scary. When we react,
simply telling our child to do what they're told, we often miss the
opportunity to connect with our child and see the world through
their eyes. As adults, it doesn't even occur to us that there could
be a monster under our bed, so we usually don't think about our
kids having those fears, either.

   In this case, Dad started going in with his daughter at
bedtime to help her calm down her body to go to sleep. As a
result, instead of popping out of bed eight or more times a night,
Mandy was now asleep within ten minutes. Dad changed his
behavior after recognizing Mandy's need. Her need needed to be
acknowledged, and the behavior went away on its own as a result
of him meeting that expressed need. This father still held his
limit that his daughter needed to go to bed, but he found a way to
meet her need in the process.

   It is easy to take our children's behavior personally. It is
easy to say that the temper tantrum is a reflection on us as

parents, especially when it happens in public, because we feel like others will judge us based upon what they see. In reality, our child's behavior is about our child and where they are on their own life journey (as is the behavior of those people we feel are judging us). Our reaction to their behavior is about our own unmet needs, our unheard feelings. Our past experiences have a strong influence over how we interpret what our children do and say. If we aren't aware of our past experiences, if we aren't aware that our own reaction is out of proportion with the actual experience, we will be unable to fully see the child and the situation in front of us as it truly is. And we'll miss the opportunity to connect with our child in the here and now—the only time we ever really have.

Those everyday experiences with your child can teach you more about yourself than anything else. Embrace the opportunities!

Questions to Ponder

- How were boundaries and limits enforced when you were growing up? How did you feel about it?

- What comes up for you when you think about discipline? What did discipline mean when you were growing up? What did it mean for your partner? What does it mean for you now as a parent?

- What are your biggest challenges regarding boundaries? Do you try to control and micromanage? Do you let your children do what they want? Or are you able to set limits while respecting feelings?

- Think of a situation where a limit is needed for your child. How does your child feel at that time? How do you feel? What is your need in this situation? What is your child's need? What can you do to meet everyone's needs in this situation?

Chapter Nine

Connecting in Community, Connecting to Ourselves

Principle 8: No man is an island. We need to create communities of support for ourselves and for our children. We need to take care of ourselves so that we can take care of our children.

Going It Alone: What Happens Without Community

For most of history, people have lived in groups that included extended families. These people worked together, played together, and shared the life cycle together with rituals throughout the day, week, and year. They raised children together, they mourned with each other over losses, and they celebrated each other's successes.

In stark contrast, most of today's families are relatively isolated. Many people do not even know their neighbors, much less talk to them or rely upon them for support. Many families are far away from their extended family, and rare are those who have grandparents living even in the same town. Even those adults with parents nearby may not have their parents' full support, especially if the adult children are parenting their children differently than the way their parents raised them. Even fully supportive grandparents are not involved in the daily life of most families, except in rare cases. The reality is that parents (and many times just one parent) are responsible for a long list of projects, events, and tasks, including caring for the children, that would overwhelm anyone. Many parents feel like there is something wrong with them when they can't keep up with everything.

One mom I worked with was feeling really overwhelmed and very down on herself because she was feeling that way. I asked her to list what she was doing on a daily basis. (You might try the same thing. Be sure your list includes those things that you need to do, but didn't get to. Those undone tasks also take up emotional energy.) This mom had an eight-year-old daughter, six-year-old son, three-year-old son, and four-month-old daughter, and her husband traveled two to three nights per week. Her list:

Get up at six in the morning (if the baby slept that long), feed the baby, get dressed. (Shower? Ha ha.) Make coffee, wake up the three older children to get them ready for school. Have breakfast. Get all children packed up and drive the two oldest to school and the three-year-old to morning preschool. Run errands, pick up preschooler on way back home in time for the baby's nap. During naptime, do laundry, clean the house, spend time with the preschooler, and possibly take a shower. After the baby's nap, feed the baby and make lunch for herself and preschooler.

I was already tired at this point, and I was only reading the list. But this mom's day wasn't even half over yet. Here is what the second half of her day looked like:

Clean up from lunch, start another load of laundry, fold and put away the first load, load the dishwasher. Spend some time with the baby. Pack everyone up to go get the older children from school. Return home for playtime, snacks, and homework; the baby's second nap falls in the middle of this. Feed the baby. Soccer practice or game three nights per week. Come back, make dinner, run dishwasher. Start getting kids ready for bed—baths, pajamas, teeth brushed, stories. Feed the baby, unload dishwasher, and collapse on the couch with a glass of wine to watch a show before crashing at 9 P.M.

What's the parent-child ratio for this mom's day? One to four for most of it: one emotionally tired adult caregiver to four children, three of whom are age six and under. When all of her activities are listed out like this, do we wonder why she was having a hard time?

We simply cannot do everything that is on our list of things to do *and* care for the children in the way they need to be cared for. It isn't that any one person is incapable, but rather that the job is too important to be left to just one person.

The ideal ratio for children under six years old is *at least* four emotionally mature adult caregivers to one child. Children with trauma histories, disrupted beginnings and special needs often have an emotional age that is less than six years old, and they have the same requirements, even if they are chronologically fourteen. Once they are more than a few months old, our children need relationships with multiple people who respect them and value them. These people can be mentors, teachers, neighbors, relatives, or our friends. The important thing is to have these other people in your children's life and to create a larger social network for your family.

When we are in relationship with other healthy individuals, we are healthy. When we are isolated and trying to do everything ourselves, we are almost certainly going to struggle.

Consciously Creating Community Support

How can families foster a supportive local community so that parents aren't alone with all of the incredible responsibilities of parenting in the twenty-first century? We first need to recognize that we need to be in community with others, as we may not have had a community experience when we were growing up. Not having a model of what this looks like creates its own set of challenges. It reminds me a bit of the 2002 film *My Big Fat Greek Wedding,* when the young man from a small, quiet, middle-class white family marries into a large, loud Greek family. It was so different from what he was used to, but he adjusted and learned to enjoy the companionship and idiosyncrasies of community life.

When I read the book *The Continuum Concept* by Jean Leidloff, I caught a glimpse of what living in a community might be like. At the same time, I was frustrated because it seemed impossible to create a support network such as the ones found in more primitive societies. I wasn't ready to give up my entire lifestyle and move to the jungle, so I started looking to see what else I could do where I live.

One idea I found was intentional communities, where people create or move to a place where everyone shares in the work of the community. They make dinners together, children play together, errands are shared, and there is regular opportunity for conversations with other adults. My heart sang as I read about the idea, and I longed for that sort of connection and community. However, my husband did not share my enthusiasm, commenting about the lack of garage for his car and tools in such communities. So I went back to the drawing board.

Some of the key elements of intentional communities got me thinking a bit more. Where could I find other like-minded parents to have conversations about parenting with and who would like to get our children together to play? Since I had young children at the time, I decided to see what local family support groups were available to me. La Leche League, Attachment Parenting International, Families for Conscious Living, Holistic Moms Network, and Mothers of Preschoolers (MOPS) were just a few that I found on my search. I found that the website *Mothering.com* had a "Community" online-forums section, with a subforum called "Finding Your Tribe," where parents could meet other like-minded, thinking parents in their local area. Through the Internet, I connected with two wonderful families I probably wouldn't have otherwise found, though they lived within five miles of my house. Other families have met other like-minded parents through churches, community events, and schools. When you start to look, you will start to find!

Many of us don't know our neighbors. Interestingly, I have found that when I make the effort to reach out to those around me, possibilities become apparent. About the same time that we moved into our house, a couple moved in a few houses down from us. Upon talking with the husband, I learned that he really enjoyed being with children and missed his nieces and nephews "back home." As the couple didn't have any children of their own yet, he asked if my older son wanted to join him for his afternoon runs with his dog. My son looked forward to this time riding his bike with another adult who respected him, and my neighbor got some company. It was win-win.

Families who have children with special needs are often especially challenged when it comes to creating a community. I encourage these families, who need specially skilled people to care for their children, to remember all of the non-child-related tasks that must be done on a daily and weekly basis. Reaching out to churches, neighbors, friends, and other community organizations for help with meals, snacks, housework, and adult conversation might be a more realistic place to start.

What stops us from reaching out? I've been surveying the parents in my phone and in-person classes, and this is what they've said:

- "I don't know how to ask for support."
- "I don't have anyone to ask."
- "I don't want to inconvenience someone else."
- "I should be able to do this myself."
- "I don't know what to ask for."
- "I don't have the time or energy right now to do a favor in return."
- "I don't have the money to pay someone to help."

What a list! How do we overcome these barriers? In one of my classes, each parent chose someone in their community that they could ask for something. And each family chose another family that they could also do something nice for. One dad showed up at a friend's house, where things had been pretty hard lately, with a pizza for the family. One mom decided to call another mom and just check on her once a day over the phone. Tori, a single mom, asked another family if they could have a weekly get-together with their two families. Little by little, the families learned to reach out to others in their own communities and began to see the rich benefits of creating a support network for themselves and their families.

The most important ingredient here is that *you* are willing to reach out and look for others. You don't know what is out there if you're not looking. Maybe that neighbor you've only briefly greeted has been looking for an opportunity to volunteer! We can all learn to seek support in ways we previously haven't.

The Importance of Self-Care

We attachment parents, including me, worry that we're not going to meet one of our child's needs and our child will be scarred for life. As a result, we are usually so focused on meeting our children's needs that we neglect our own.

But perhaps our child will be scarred because we aren't meeting our own needs. Our children need us to be available to take care of them, but we cannot take care of them if our own needs aren't being met. The more dysregulated we are, the more we need external structure for ourselves. Trauma and unmet needs from our early lives, along with our current level of stress, will create more chaos in our bodies. But when we take time for ourselves, everything seems to go more smoothly. We're more able to handle the difficulties that come about during our day with greater ease.

What do we need to do to take better care of our own needs and thus take better care of our children? What are doable suggestions and guidelines that can help our decision-making and help us better meet our own needs?

If you're completely overwhelmed, concentrate on the following three core tasks and get help with them if necessary:

- sleeping at regular times
- eating at regular times
- exercising

These simple things are often the first to go when we get overwhelmed, yet they are the foundation of our overall health.

Sleeping can sometimes be a challenge when we have so many demands on our time. This is never more true that when we have a new baby. If you have a new baby, it may mean that you need to nap when baby naps instead of cleaning. If your baby is waking frequently and disturbing your sleep, go to bed earlier for a little while and sleep whenever your baby sleeps. The rest of the housework can and will wait. Seek help from your partner, family, friends, or neighbors for those extra things that can be done by someone else for a short time. If the birth was traumatic, consider that you may need some additional support to move through and integrate the experience. This will help everyone to sleep better.

Those with children out of babyhood may also find that their to-do list is what keeps them up at night. One of the best gifts we can give our families is to get enough sleep when possible. (We'll be talking about this hot topic again in Books II, III, and IV.)

Eating was usually the first thing to go for me when I got stressed out as a new parent. I was home, mostly alone, with our son. He was a colicky baby, and after I laid him down contentedly somewhere, I rarely had more than a minute before he was back up and needing my attention. I recognize now that I was in survival (red-light) mode, and I wasn't taking care of my body's need for good food. I was also nursing what seemed at the time to be 24/7, so I needed more food than normal. My husband and I started putting together snacks in the fridge the night before—snacks that I could easily grab with one hand—so that I could still manage to eat throughout the day. Make sure your diet isn't composed of potato chips and chocolate-chip cookies for optimal results. (We tend to crave sweet, salty, or fatty foods when we're stressed. One mom in one of my classes proclaimed to have found the perfect food for her stressed out states: a Snickers bar. It met all the requirements!)

When my children were older and I found myself yet again in a survival mode, I had some friends help me make meals that could go in the freezer. Then, at dinnertime, I could just pull out a frozen meal and heat it up quickly rather than attempting to make food with dysregulated children underfoot. Also, do what you need to do to make sure that meals are served at regular times. Your body and your family will thank you.

Exercise is one of those things that, as children, we either had modeled for us or we didn't. If we didn't have the templates for exercise when we were growing up, regular exercise requires dedication and commitment—and, in my own case, an exercise-accountability partner. Exercise of any form helps to regulate the body, especially if we can find a time to exercise consistently. Even a ten-minute daily walk can help to ease stress.

In addition to sleep, regular meals, and exercise, connecting with ourselves, our primary parenting partner, and our family and friends will help us maintain the inner balance we need to remain calm and present for our children. This includes expressing feelings with someone who can be present with us, as well as expressing our thoughts. Sometimes we fall into either just expressing our feelings or being stuck in our heads with our thoughts. Connecting in this way is deeper than just telling someone about our day.

Time to Take Care of Ourselves

Few people disagree with the notion that taking care of ourselves is important. In fact, most of us usually get excited when we start talking about meeting our own needs. But most people don't take the time to actually do it. There are too many other demands that need to take precedence.

I suggest that we don't have the time to *not* take this time. I also suggest that self-care doesn't have to take an hour or two on a daily basis. If you haven't been taking any time at all for yourself, spending only five or ten minutes a day is a wonderful place to start. Taking just a few minutes for yourself is enough to start creating a new, healthy habit.

Some parents wake up a few minutes before the children to get this time. Others designate the first few minutes after the children have gone off to school, before they get started with their workday or housework. Some parents find the time after the children are in bed to be a good opportunity to have a little time by themselves. Picking a consistent time for self-care generally works better than something more sporadic, but different family situations offer different options. Someone with a newborn who hasn't normalized his or her bodily rhythms yet is in a very different situation than another parent who has teenagers in school, and both of these situations look very different than that of a mom homeschooling children between the ages of four and fifteen! You have to figure out what will work best for you and your family situation.

One homeschooling family with three daughters between the ages of seven and fifteen decided that the best way to make time for parental self-care was to have designated time off. They discovered that when the mom, Sue, was home, the kids went to her even if Larry, the dad, was there and available. So now, every Wednesday evening, Sue heads out to do something nurturing for herself. These days, she's spending her time painting and creating mosaics at a community art center or getting together with her other mom friends. Larry's night off is Monday, and he often goes to take a class through his church or heads down to a friend's house to unwind. As the girls have grown older, Sue has made the time to invite one girl at a time to join her while she paints or creates mosaics and lets them create their own special project. This way, they can see and experience firsthand self-nurturing, and they have a much better idea of what their mother is doing when she is away. Larry has also started inviting one girl at a time to join him for a class through his church when there is something age appropriate. Good self-care won't be a mystery to these girls!

Another mother, Brenda, was thoroughly captivated by Janet Conner's *Writing Down Your Soul* book and its exploration of writing as a spiritual practice, and she really wanted to make writing a priority in her life. She had two small boys at home with her and really struggled to figure out when she was going to have the time to write. Finally, it dawned on her that she could just start having a daily family writing time. She gave both of her boys, ages two and four, a journal just like hers and some special crayons, and they each took the time to write each night before bed. She was able to get her time to write, and her boys got the benefit of seeing her model self-care. Plus, her boys drew beautiful images during their writing time—images she was able to keep and treasure.

There are as many ways to carve out time for self-care as there are parents who need it. Talk to other families in your community and ask when and how they get their own needs met. You just might hear an idea that inspires you!

Time to Connect to Our Self and Our Inner Guidance System

In her book *Connection Parenting*, Pam Leo has a wonderful description of why it is so important to take time to recharge ourselves, and it involves our brain-wave states. When we are alert, active, and thinking, we are in the beta brain-wave state.

Many parents spend time in this state all day long, until their heads hit the pillow at night; they live their entire days moving from task to task and solving problems. But there are three other brain-wave states that are very important for our overall health. Delta is the brain-wave state associated with a deep sleep, which we all need at least from time to time. Alpha is a relaxed state that we would be in when we are meditating, walking in nature, painting a picture, playing a musical instrument, knitting, or listening to soothing music; many parents stop doing these things because there is little time and other things take the priority. Theta is an even deeper state of relaxation in which we can access our intuition, inspiration, creativity, and novel solutions.

We are more patient when we have had time to relax into a brain-wave state other than beta. And if we are parenting in a way that is different than the way we were raised, it is even more important to be able to access theta because so many of us have disconnected from our internal guidance systems. You have the answers to your own parenting challenges and questions within you; you just need to learn how to access those answers.

Janet Conner's book *Writing Down Your Soul* explains a wonderful process that allows anyone to access the theta brain-wave state and can really help you connect with your inner guidance system. (More about the "Writing Down Your Soul" process can be found in the resources section in this book and in the audio interview I did with Janet Conner in 2008.) Parents report seeing big changes in their family when they start connecting with themselves and their inner guidance systems on a daily basis.

Other parents enjoy meditation, yoga, prayer, dancing, singing, connecting with a friend, or just sitting quietly for a few minutes outside. Whatever activity you choose, taking even just ten minutes a day to give yourself a break from the beta state will benefit both you and your children immensely.

Time to Connect with Your Partner

When your family has young children or older children with big needs, taking the time to connect with your parenting partner becomes even more important. I was recently talking to a couple and asked how much time they spent talking to each other during the week. After thinking about it, they said probably about ten minutes—a week! And they spent this time talking about the kids and managing their activities. No wonder they were having communication issues and weren't feeling very connected to one another!

When children are very small, it takes some creativity to connect with your partner and still respect the needs of your young children. It is ideal if we have a family member or close friend who is around frequently and is willing to babysit our children while we go out and have a date. One mom's sister lived nearby and was around all the time to watch her nephew. She watched him sometimes in the morning, when he was at his best, while his parents went out together, as he tended to be fussier and wanted his mom at night.

Other parents who don't have relatives or good friends nearby can make it a point to have a date at least one night a week after the children are in bed. One family I know made a special meal complete with candles, a clean tablecloth, and cloth napkins. Mom and Dad would sit up together and have a grown-up meal, enjoying their time with one another.

Also make it a point to connect with each other during the day to talk about something not related to family maintenance. It is easy to get sucked into the trap of talking only about the kids. Parents need time to be people, too. And it is critically important that at least some of this time is spent connecting on an emotional level and sharing your feelings about parenting. (If you need some help getting started, I highly suggest checking out Hedy Schleifer's work at http://www.hedyyumi.com.) Partners need to create emotional safety and be able to move into emotional territory together in order to really feel connected. But most of us don't know how to do that. "Our children live in the space between us," as Hedy says, so it is important to clear the space.

As your children grow old enough to understand that when you leave, you will come back—normally somewhere around the fourth year of life—consider adding in short trips away with your partner. If you have a child with a trauma history, the child may be much older before he or she is able to handle separations like that without going into survival mode. With those children, it isn't that you can't get away; it is just that those children need us to be mindful of their needs and feelings regarding separations.

When we reconnect with our parenting partner and prioritize that relationship, everyone is more able to meet the needs of the children.

Time to Connect with Friends and Family

Do you have a group of parents you connect with on a regular basis? For a long time, my means of connecting with other parents was meeting up with them at the park with our kids so that I could socialize. I think it probably saved my sanity to be able to do that and find others who understood my parenting struggles and victories. Some families have extended family gatherings on a regular basis to share what is going on in their lives.

If you are a single parent, it is vital to find a group of friends or family members who understand you and can offer you support. Make the time to connect with others who can offer a helping hand if you are feeling overwhelmed, but who can also provide connection to others.

We also need time to connect with the larger community. For some people, this community means church. For others, it might mean the community of the school their children attend. Perhaps it is a neighborhood group that you start to create

connections with children and parents who have similar inter-
ests. Or maybe it is a book club that meets to discuss the con-
cepts in Pam Leo's *Connection Parenting* or those in this book.
Or perhaps your support group is one connected with Attachment Parenting International. One woman in Indiana took my
DVD *Parenting Beyond Behaviors* and, with permission, showed
it to the parents involved in her local parenting support group.
They were able to discuss the ideas of the eight principles of
conscious parenting together and support each other as they
implemented the ideas.

When we start connecting with our communities
in meaningful ways, we can further expand on parenting
ideas and will find ourselves having more support for our
parenting philosophy.

Questions to Ponder

- Did someone you know model connecting with the self
  and the inner guidance system when you were a child, or
  is this idea brand new to you? Do you already take time
  to reconnect with your inner self or not?

- Do you have a community of like-minded people in your
  life? Who are your biggest supporters?

- Do you take time for self-care? Find one thing you'd be
  willing to try this next week to take care of yourself.

Conclusion

As parents, we have a steady diet of conflicting information coming at us from all directions. The long list of essential dos and don'ts has most of us spinning our wheels in indecision, not knowing what we're actually supposed to do to parent our children. We follow parenting advice from "experts" even if it doesn't feel right because we aren't sure what else to do or we feel that someone else must know what our child needs better than we do.

Consciously Parenting is about listening to your own inner guidance system, trusting your own inner voice about what is needed in your family and for your child. It is also about finding what you need and finding a way to meet your own needs in a way that still respects the needs of your child and the needs of the relationship.

Consciously Parenting gives us a compass and a map to help guide us on our parenting journey with 8 guiding principles based on current science, using intuition as our guide. No one knows our child the way we do and yet we're so close to our own children that we can't always see the bigger picture. Consciously Parenting is about gaining a different vantage point and remembering that the most important thing we can do as a parent is to focus on the relationship.

We're going to make mistakes. And that's OK. Actually, "mistakes" allow us the opportunity to reconnect and repair the relationship when there has been a disconnection, which is a critical part of attachment. Sometimes *we* will reach out to reconnect and sometimes it will be our child. And sometimes it will take a while before we can see that our own story is getting in the way of reconnecting.

Parenting is a journey, not a destination. We'll take "wrong turns" and end up in scary back alleys, but we need to remember that it is only a wrong turn if we don't learn from it.

Eventually. Lessons will be repeated until learned and parenting does a great job of providing opportunities for us to learn.

We become parents because we want to have a loving connection with our children. We want to feel joy and wonder and we become frustrated when we feel anger, resentment, confusion or pain, when we see our child is suffering and we don't know how to help her. Or maybe we're aware that we are the one in pain. When we begin to focus on the communication behind the behaviors, we begin to see our child in a new light. And we begin to understand ourselves more deeply. Parenting becomes a gift, a treasure.

In Book II of the Consciously Parenting series, we're going to be taking a closer look at Consciously Creating Healthy Relationships by looking at the beginning of life and how our parenting decisions impact the relationship. We'll be looking more closely at the early years of life and how events during early life can have a profound effect on our patterns and the way we view our world. We'll also be looking at how those patterns can be shifted when things didn't get off to a good start for one reason or another. Even if your children are no longer babies or toddlers, Book II is essential for understanding more about yourself and your children. Stay tuned for more information coming soon at consciouslyparenting.com!

Best wishes on your parenting journey!

Resources

Books

<u>Affect Dysregulation and Disorders of the Self</u> by Allan N. Schore

<u>Attached at the Heart: 8 Proven Parenting Principles for Raising Connected and Compassionate Children</u> by Barbara Nicholson and Lysa Parker

<u>Becoming Attached: First Relationships and How They Shape Our Capacity to Love</u> by Robert Karen

<u>Biology of Belief</u> by Bruce Lipton

<u>The Boy Who Was Raised as a Dog</u> by Bruce Perry

<u>Connection Parenting: Parenting through Connection instead of Coercion, Through Love instead of Fear</u> by Pam Leo, website: www.connectionparenting.com

<u>The Continuum Concept</u> by Jean Liedloff

<u>The Family Bed</u> by Tine Thevenin

<u>Healing Trauma: Attachment, Mind, Body, and Brain</u>, Edited by Marion F. Solomon and Daniel J. Siegel

<u>The Healing Power of Emotion: Affective Neuroscience, Development, and Clinical Practice</u>, Edited by Diana Fosha, Daniel J. Siegel, and Marion F. Solomon

<u>Hold Me Tight: Seven Conversations for a Lifetime of Love</u> by Dr. Sue Johnson, website: www.iceeft.com

Immaculate Deception II: Myth, Magic, and Birth by Suzanne Arms, website: www.birthingthefuture.org

Keeping the Love You Find: A Personal Guide by Harville Hendrix

Let the Baby Drive: Navigating the Road of New Motherhood by Lu Hanessian, websites: www.letthebabydrive.com, and www.parent2parentu.com

The Making and Breaking of Affectional Bonds by John Bowlby

Molecules of Emotion: Why You Feel the Way You Feel by Candace B. Pert, PhD

The Neurobiology of "We": How Relationships, the Mind, and the Brain Interact to Shape Who We Are by Daniel Seigel (audio book)

Opening Up: The Healing Power of Expressing Emotions by James Pennebaker

Parenting From the Inside Out: How a Deeper Self-Understanding Can Help You Raise Children Who Thrive by Daniel J. Siegel and Mary Hartzell

Playing in the Unified Field: Raising and Becoming Conscious, Creative Human Beings by Carla Hannaford

Raising Our Children, Raising Ourselves: Transforming parent-child relationships from reaction and struggle to freedom, power and joy by Naomi Aldort

Real Love by Greg Baer

The Science of Parenting: How today's brain research can help you raise happy, emotionally balanced children by Margot Sunderland

Three in a Bed: The Benefits of Sleeping With Your Baby by Deborah Jackson

Trauma Through a Child's Eyes: Awakening the Ordinary Miracle of Healing by Peter A Levine and Maggie Kline

Waking the Tiger: Healing Trauma by Peter Levine

Why Love Matters: How Affection Shapes a Baby's Brain by Sue Gerhardt

The Womanly Art of Breastfeeding published by La Leche League, website: www.llli.org

Writing Down Your Soul: How to Activate and Listen to the Extraordinary Voice Within by Janet Conner, website www.writingdownyoursoul.com

You Can Heal Your Life by Louise Hay

Additional Resources

Attachment Parenting International, website www.attachmentparenting.org

Carrie Contey, website www.slowfamilyliving.com

Hedy Schleifer, LMHC, website: www.hedyyumi.com

Holistic Moms Network, website www.holisticmoms.org

Infant Massage USA, website www.infantmassageusa.org

International Chiropractic Pediatric Association, website: icpa4kids.com

Interview with Janet Conner: www.consciouslyparenting.com/teleseminars/JanetConner1.php

Kindred Community, website www.kindredcommunity.com

La Leche League International, website www.llli.org

Mothering Magazine, website www.mothering.com

Parenting Beyond Behaviors DVD Set by Rebecca Thompson: www.consciouslyparenting.com/store/pbb.php

Pathways to Family Wellness Magazine, website www.pathwaystofamilywellness.org

Ray Castellino and Mary Jackson, *Little People, Big Challenges*. www.consciouslyparenting.com/LPBC
Website: www.aboutconnections.com

William Sears, MD. Website: www.askdrsears.com

Reactive Attachment Disorder Resources:

Dr. Daniel Amen, Amen Clinics: http://www.amenclinics.net

Eric Guy, Center for Victory: www.centerforvictory.com

Dr. Bruce Perry, The Boy Who Was Raised as a Dog, www.childtrauma.org

Karyn Purvis: http://empoweredtoconnect.org